DUGOURC: A Garden Scene

FRENCH DRAWINGS
OF THE
EIGHTEENTH
CENTURY

by

DENYS SUTTON

LONDON : PLEIADES BOOKS : MCMXLIX

FOR

SONJA

FIRST PUBLISHED 1949
BY PLEIADES BOOKS LTD 11 FITZROY SQUARE LONDON W1
PRINTED IN GREAT BRITAIN
BY THE SHENVAL PRESS LONDON AND HERTFORD

PREFACE

★

THE AIM of this volume is not to supply a detailed examination of the French draughtsmen of the eighteenth century; such a volume would necessarily be specialist in its appeal and, as such, outside the scope of this series. It is rather to give some idea of the general development of the fine arts in France during the eighteenth century, with special emphasis on the drawings of the period, and to suggest something of the atmosphere of the cultural background.

This volume is in a large measure the result of my years as an undergraduate at Oxford, when, though I should perhaps have been reading for Schools, I had the opportunity to study in the Ashmolean Museum. My gratitude to Dr K. T. Parker, the Keeper of this Museum, for stimulating my interest in drawings, is great. The book itself was written, however, after the war and the difficulties of assembling the photographic material have been considerable.

I should like to thank Monsieur and Madame Jean Adhémar, Mr John Nicholas Brown, Mr D. Carne-Ross, Dr Edith Hoffmann, Dr K. T. Parker, Mr Ian Robertson, Mr John Russell, Dr Alfred Scharf, Mr Anthony Sutton, Miss Penelope Tremayne, Dr A. B. de Vries, Mr Francis Watson and Mr George Wildenstein, for help in various ways. My thanks are also due to the staff of museums and institutions in England and abroad and to many collectors and dealers for assistance. Above all, I should thank my parents for their understanding and generosity.

DENYS SUTTON

London, 1948

CONTENTS

LIST OF PLATES

COLOUR PLATES

MONOCHROME PLATES

I. BACKGROUND TO A CENTURY

OF RECENT YEARS, French art of the eighteenth century has suffered a decline in popular esteem in this country. The names of its greatest artists continue to be repeated with respect. Yet the view is often expressed, or at any rate hinted, that an age so corrupt in its morals and so polished in its manners was incapable of producing an art deserving the respect of a generation, such as our own, which prides itself on the seriousness of its motives and is only too conscious of the revolutionary character of much of its own culture. For many, therefore, the eighteenth century appears under its more questionable aspects, and the amusing escapades of adventurers such as Casanova, or of licentious courtiers such as the Duc de Richelieu, are wrongly considered to be characteristic of the epoch as a whole. How often, indeed, is the celebrated story of Louis XV and his alleged harem in the Parc aux Cerfs brought up as a reproach and used as a rod to belabour the century, or as the pretext for condescending patronage of a period that was as fertile as it was controversial.

Just as the pretended salaciousness of its art has contributed towards an underestimation of its virtues, the eighteenth century is suspect also because of its refusal, generally speaking, to complicate situations. The open way in which the men and women of this period revealed their motives must appear, indeed, horribly naïve and unsubtle to our generation, which is so self-conscious about its pleasures. Their very frankness and capacity for enthusiasm were combined, however, with a percipient knowledge of human motives—as they appear, at any rate, on the surface. They saw life clearly and knew the foibles of human nature. They were not afraid to follow facts to their ultimate conclusions, and the aristocracy's dabbling in the ideas of the 'Philosophes' contributed to the Revolution of 1789 and to its own downfall. What is so fascinating about the society described by Crébillon, Chevrier, Prévost and many others, is the determination of its members to extract the maximum pleasure from life. They were realists. Life had to be faced, to be enjoyed while it could, and then—well, as the Cardinal Bernis wrote:

> 'Pour éterniser sa mémoire,
> On perd des moments les plus doux:
> Pourquoi chercher si loin la gloire?
> Le plaisir est si près de nous.' [1]

This ability to enjoy its pleasures and also, one may at times suspect, its misfortunes, gave the eighteenth century much of its flavour and character. It set itself an aim, the pursuit of Happiness, the eternal 'Bonheur', and if it chose to seek it in precise, as well as in philosophic, terms, who can be surprised? It had always the consolation, too, of contemplating the comedy of manners and of attempting to distil in aphoristic form a profound and varied knowledge of life. 'How exquisitely ironic,' Logan Pearsall Smith once wrote, 'is

B   1

the entertainment we can derive from our disillusions.' The men and women of the eighteenth century would surely have subscribed to this charming conceit: however disillusioned they may have been, however bored by the spectacle of Vanity Fair, they were serious in so far as they were positive; for all their scepticism, they believed in life. It is perhaps for this reason that the eighteenth century seems so satisfactory; it was so complete, so well rounded.

Why, one wonders, has the eighteenth century and so much of its art been dismissed as frivolous? This conception results perhaps from the interpretation of two late nineteenth-century writers, Edmond and Jules de Goncourt. They themselves did not hold such views: they were too steeped in, and too devoted to, the century to travesty its qualities. Yet, because the Goncourts devoted the major part of their writing and research to certain aspects of the period, the position of the royal mistresses and of the great actresses, such as La Guimard, La Clairon and Sophie Arnould, in the society of their time, the age itself has often been seen exclusively from their special point of view. Their particular interpretation has been over-simplified and vulgarized by later generations; the Rococo has too often been equated with frivolity. The figures they described were important, however, because they exerted so profound and generally so beneficial an influence on contemporary culture; their private lives were relevant because they were on intimate terms with the principal figures of the age. But, as Edmond de Goncourt shrewdly observed in concluding his biography of Madame de Pompadour, time has veiled the weaknesses of the woman: her feminine charm still captivates, but she is principally remembered as a great and understanding patron of the arts. The Goncourts, indeed, were no escapists seeking a rose-coloured dream in the art and manners of the past. Their novel of contemporary life, *Manette Salomon*, reveals a deep understanding of the psychological motivations of the female mind at its most disconcerting. In their historical writings, the Goncourts not only sought to re-create the personalities of the women of the past: they wished to communicate to their contemporaries their own excitement in rediscovering an art and a civilization which had been too long neglected. '*Pour cette histoire, il nous a fallu découvrir,*' they said, '*les nouvelles sources du Vrai, demander nos documents aux journaux, aux brochures, à tout ce monde de papier mort et méprisé jusqu'ici, aux autographes, aux gravures, aux dessins, aux tableaux, à tous les monuments intimes, qu'une époque laisse derrière elle pour être sa confession et sa résurrection.*'[2]

The Goncourts were lucky in their period. They began their work at a time when the eighteenth century was only just beginning to emerge from neglect. They participated in that great movement of historical writing which numbered Michelet and de Tocqueville amongst its adherents. Until then, people had tended to discredit the art of the preceding century; its tastes and views seemed too dissimilar from their own. The many roots which nineteenth-century Romanticism had in the previous era were not immediately apparent; they had to wait their time until they received due examination. Under the First Empire a connoisseur such as Vivant-Denon attempted to preserve the art and the gracious ways of the *Ancien Régime*, but he was in a minority. Collectors anxious to possess examples of eighteenth-century art were few, though by the middle of the century men such as Rochard, the miniaturist, and Lord Hertford had taken advantage of the favourable circumstances and formed important collections of eighteenth-century art. Prices were low and good pictures easy to find.[3] With the Second Empire, the eighteenth century enjoyed a revival of interest: the viewpoints of both generations were similar in so many respects. It was the role of the Goncourts to appear at this moment, compress into their writings all the available knowledge and diffuse amongst the many a taste which had previously been the concern of only a few. They and their contemporaries were the predecessors of the great collectors and connoisseurs, such as Beurdeley and Chennevières, Dormeuil and Strauss, not to mention the many historians and dealers who have devoted their attention to this fascinating century.

To study the period without constant reference to the Goncourts would be to miss much of its spirit and, moreover, to forgo an enjoyable experience. A judgment based on their views alone, on the other hand, would necessarily deny a state of affairs which they took for granted: that a rich and aristocratic society was balanced by a poor and unjustly treated lower class. The background of the age was not only Versailles and the Rue St Honoré: it was the quartier St Antoine, the poverty-stricken countryside and the social injustices of a society based on excessive privilege. Poverty bit deep. Yet, however important such departments of the social system may be for the student of history proper or for the propagandist, they touch only lightly on the art of the period. Its artists came, it is true, mainly from the middle or lower classes, but its patrons belonged to the aristocracy or to the rich *bourgeoisie*. Towards the end, art may have been imbued with a moral fervour, with David to round off the century, but in its most typical moments it expressed the way of life of an easy and affluent society. However brutal and hard the period may appear in some of its aspects, it was gracious and civilized in many others. It was very French in so far as it was very paradoxical. It was sceptical yet enthusiastic. It was marked, indeed, by one particular quality which may seem at variance with the rules of Reason themselves: it was passionate in its approach to art, to thought and to life.

The spirit and the manners of the age itself are extremely well reflected in the drawing which reveals qualities in the period which would not perhaps transpire from a study of its painting or sculpture alone. The drawing, indeed, ideally illuminates the mind of an epoch as well as of an artist. The drawing shows the artist in the throes of composition, as he is rejecting or utilizing various aspects of visual experience. The artist at times is seen jotting down his first warm and spontaneous impressions of a subject, at others working out a composition. Drawings indicate sides of an artist's personality which we might suspect, but of which we could never be certain unless, as in the case of Raphael or Leonardo, they were present to supplement our exiguous knowledge. They aid in the formation of a full appreciation of an artist's style; so often a painter who seems cold and academic, utterly uninspired in his painting, gains a sort of warmth, even a touch of passion, in the act of drawing. Self-consciousness then disappears: his formal self is discarded to reveal a freshness which in turn is killed when he attempts to create in a more grandiloquent manner. Rubens was far from being an academic painter, but there is a description of him drawing by a seventeenth-century English writer which helps to explain that tempestuous immediacy which distinguishes his sketches. He would 'sit musing upon his work for some time,' wrote William Sanderson,[4] 'and even in an instant in the liveliness of spirit, with nimble hand would force his over-charged brain into description, as not to be contained in the compass of ordinary practice, but a violent driving on of the passion.' Just this quality of an almost spontaneous combustion of temperament is to be found in the drawings of the best masters; therein lies their perennial fascination.

The eighteenth century was well served by its draughtsmen. Their drawings matched the vivacious quality of the age, its lightness of touch, its desire for freedom. They formed a necessary and appropriate counterpart to the supple, vigorous prose of Voltaire or Fréron, that sharp weapon for controversy and for vivid and racy analysis which had replaced the stately periods of the preceding century. The drawing was the proper instrument, sensitive, alert and even malicious, for the record of an age that was prepared to be profound but hated to be dull. The drawing, the swift sketch, the *croqueton*, was exactly the right medium for the *Dessinateur des Menus Plaisirs*, such as Cochin or Moreau, to jot down his impressions of royal ceremonies and masked balls, to catch the image of the King at the levée attended by his courtiers or supping at Louveciennes (Pl. XXXI), or to leave exquisite notations of the beauties of the court and stage. '*On dit que l'homme est un animal sociable*,' wrote Montesquieu in one of his *Lettres Persanes*; '*sur ce pied-là, il me paraît qu'un Français est plus homme qu'un autre; c'est l'homme par excellence, car il semble être fait uniquement pour la société.*'[5] This sociability the French draughtsmen and engravers of the age reflected readily and easily in their works. They displayed, moreover, that sense of *contemporanéité*, that quick grasp of a situation or a scene which has always distinguished the French and which in the literature of this period appeared in the observations of Montesquieu, Mercier, and Rétif de la Bretonne. How right, indeed, was Edmond de Goncourt to reply when Ephrussi and Dreyfus asked him to lend some drawings to an exhibition they were organizing at the Ecole des Beaux-Arts: '*Ce n'est pas deux ou trois Watteau, Boucher, Latour qu'il me faut vous prêter. Car ce que mon frère et moi avons poursuivi avec tant de curiosité, fureté avec tant de passion, ce n'est pas tel ou tel artiste, c'est un siècle, et le plus essentiellement français de notre histoire nationale.*'[6]

The drawing was no longer exclusively considered as a preparatory sketch for another work: it had its own right to existence, its own place in the hierarchy of the arts. All that was needed was a piece of paper, plain or tinted, and the sanguine beloved of the period; a charming sketch was soon available, not to remain hidden in the artist's portfolios but, suitably framed, to ornament some boudoir or salon. The drawing was able to convey that impression of charm and elegance which was so much sought by the period. In this search, the painter and draughtsman were aided by their employment of a particular and characteristic technique, the celebrated *pierre rouge*, sanguine, red chalk, of the period. Already used by Fréminet, Callot and Bellange in the seventeenth century, in the hands of eighteenth-century artists it became endowed with a superb sense of plasticity

4

and colour, containing as it did the variations of the palette, especially if mixed with black and white chalks. To aid their attempt to endow the drawing with softness, a technique of the *dessin estompé*, or the smudged drawing, was used with particular effect by Boucher, Carle van Loo and Greuze.

Yet, for all this desire for lightness and reality, the academic teaching, especially in the first half of the century, was that of the classical period. Du Fresnoy, the theorist, for instance, recommended that an artist should draw first from the antique and then copy from renowned masters. It was Lebrun's method, and one which was followed during most of the century, that the artist should copy at first fine antiques or the paintings of Raphael, and then nature, finally drawing nature alone but with the antique or Raphael to act as a guide and measure. These precepts did not accord with those of the more individual artists of the century: Watteau was among the first to draw whatever pleased him. During the period, the artist turned for his models to real life rather than to the antique or to the works of earlier masters. Fragonard, for instance, in his tender wash drawings of rustic or gallant scenes, and Gabriel de Saint-Aubin in his delicate pencil and watercolour sketches of Paris, indicated that the artist considered contemporary society sufficient for his needs. By 1792 it was quite safe for Watelet to recommend in his *Dictionnaire des Arts* that the painter should draw directly from nature.

The tradition of fine draughtsmanship had been of long standing in France, from the Middle Ages onwards. The miniaturists, the *Maître du Coeur d'Amour Epris*, or Fouquet, had shown that intensity could be rendered in a minute form. Later, Clouet had revealed that the aristocratic portrait could be used to give an insight into character. The elegant mannerism of the School of Fontainebleau, on the other hand, survived in the drawings of Bellange and Callot: their incisive wit, their grace, and their use of red chalk, announced the art of Gillot and Watteau.

Throughout the period, a national tradition of painting was constantly endeavouring to make its appearance. Italianism, as such, had reached its apogee with the visit of Bernini to France in 1665, though already the particular qualities of Italian art had been digested and transposed by Poussin into a style that was essentially French. Poussin himself is an artist of rhythm. He abounds in sensibility. Many of his paintings display a certain mechanism: the lack of contact, of harmony between the figures and their landscape background, is apt to disturb. But in those paintings where the units are submerged in the whole, where he succeeds in fusing the machine with his emotional reaction, all is charged with a genial warmth. His paint is rich and sensuous, his colour reverberates with a sense of joy; the whole is welded together by a constructive composition in which, as in his *Inspiration d'un Poète* (Louvre) or his *Three Graces* (Dresden), the figures are lifted with a sense of movement anticipating Matisse.

Poussin's drawings contain a suggestion of Arcadian delight; the dancing figures, garlanded with wreaths, express an understanding, at once poignant and profound, of the venerableness of antiquity, a continuation and reminder, vivid and humanistic, of the perpetual inspiration of the classical heritage. This warm appraisal of the Bacchic elements

5

of Greece is so different from the glacial machinery of Neo-classical painting: how much more does it recall the poetry of Hölderlin and Keats. Poussin, indeed, is at once a classicist and a romantic: his works are static, yet in movement. As a draughtsman, he relied much on symbolical notation; a rapid turn of the pen and a face was indicated. His great contemporary, Claude, used a rather similar approach. The artist of the *genius loci*, as Roger Fry once so felicitously termed him, he was at his most accomplished and his most complete in his pure landscape drawings of the environs of Rome. Brilliant, sensitive and direct, he brought to French draughtsmanship that firm view of nature which has always proved one of its lasting sources of inspiration; that evocation of the very wetness of water, the mystery of pools, which appears with particular and insistent delicacy in his celebrated drawing of *The Tiber above Rome* in the British Museum.

Much draughtsmanship of the seventeenth century, however, lacked this warmth and directness. Bold and accomplished though it was, it had no inner conviction; it relied too much on the formulae of the Italians. Its heaviness resulted perhaps from its utilitarian nature: more often than not, it was destined as a preparatory sketch for some painting. If today the drawings of Eustache Le Sueur seem painfully pedestrian, in the eighteenth century they seemed to so judicious a connoisseur as Mariette to represent all that was best in the Italian manner: they were in the direct line of descent from Raphael and typified that '*manière sage, pure, élevée*',[7] which to the traditionists of the period seemed lost. Such draughtsmanship was, however, the correct reflection of that official and awe-inspiring style of painting which dominated the middle years of the seventeenth century: the school of Lebrun.

The history of French painting in the second half of the seventeenth century is the history of its centralization and its submission to the ideal of Versailles. Versailles, indeed, is an artistic just as much as a political symbol. Louis XIV and his advisers considered that art should be employed, not only for its aesthetic properties, but because of its value as a means of diffusing the King's personality and power. Art, it was felt, had a part to play in celebrating the glories of his reign and the magnificence of his person. The works of the most excellent painters in the past, ran the words of Louis's patent of nobility to Lebrun, had served to embellish the palaces of Princes and as '*monuments à leur gloire, exprimants par un langage muet leurs plus belles et plus héroiques actions*'.[8]

Versailles itself was a monument to the efficacy and correctness of Louis's system; its massive forms, its noble aspect, were an artistic expression of the spirit of the century and of the royal personality. A symbol of his dignity and a triumphant expression of his authoritarian principles, Versailles successfully subordinated the genius of various artists to the demands of one man alone. It was the symbol of his orthodox conception of the State and of art, of that policy which had inspired Colbert and contributed towards the foundation of the Academy of Painting.

The style that accompanied this architectural triumph met the needs of one man and one element alone: the King and the State. There was much that was noble about it; yet it demanded, and had to receive, the collaboration of circumstances. Once the conditions of its success were removed, its possible pretentiousness became apparent. If the standards of taste and of manners changed, the great decorative tradition was likely to end in stultification. Within the orbit of the Crown, and of the Crown at its most splendid, it was superb; for a private person who was not a king it was unsuited, even unnecessary. But this style contained few elements likely to appeal to the rich nobility and to the financiers who were gradually growing in importance. The private patron was eager for paintings that would provide a charming background to life. Inevitably, the days of the Grand Manner were numbered. The conditions of life had themselves altered. Society was moving away from its absorption in the person of the Monarchy. The wounds of the Fronde had been healed, and the forms of life tended to swing back into individualism and decentralization. Power was to remain in the hands of the throne, but the ability of an absolutist idea to impose itself was beginning to be challenged. How far such political, economic and social changes affected the nature of painting is difficult to determine unless the historian is content to adopt those criteria in accordance with which all productions of the human spirit are assessed by their material considerations. Yet the interdependence of art and society was evident. However much artists may have wished to continue painting in the tradition of grand decoration, and few perhaps did, the changing conditions of the country, the pressure of economic events, and the emergence of a new class of patrons, necessitated style itself to adopt new forms and means.

The last years of Louis XIV's reign were, indeed, to witness a different sort of life from that of the immediate past. The contrast is striking. The splendour that shone on the country in its prime had been dimmed by the prostrating effect of war and financial disaster. The King himself was no longer the *Roi Soleil*. Middle-aged and disillusioned, he was content to seek in the domesticity provided by Madame de Maintenon a substitute for the excitement that had radiated from Mlle de Montespan. Yet even in these dismal years, Louis still maintained his grasp on affairs; there was no weakening of his vigilant eye. What is so interesting and so important about this last period is, that it was then that those elements which were to constitute the style of the eighteenth century began to show themselves as other than scattered tendencies. Both politically and artistically, the representatives of the younger generation waited at Meudon or at Paris, to take control.

There was no specific breakaway from the art of the past, no one moment when it was possible to affirm that a new manner of painting had begun. During those years between the death of Lebrun, in 1690, and that of Watteau, in 1721, various currents of tastes and styles of painting existed side by side. The change was foreshadowed in painting before it actually took place. That a reaction against the Absolutist ideas of Lebrun should have occurred was perhaps inevitable. It forms, indeed, part of the French tradition, that one style should react against another, that Poussin should be balanced by Watteau and Watteau by David, in the same way as the analytical character of Cézanne was completed and carried one stage further by the Fauves and the Cubists. The signs of this reaction, this swing of the pendulum, were not far to seek: in the painting of Mignard, in the quarrel between the Ancients and Moderns, in the controversy between the Poussinistes

7

and the Rubenistes. This struggle broke out, paradoxically enough, in the Academy itself, where it was waged between rival theorists. It was the clash between the idea of Progress, which was to be one of the principal themes of the eighteenth century, and of an adherence to the ideals of the Ancients, a concept which was to reappear at the end of the century. The nature of this celebrated, though now dusty, controversy has been well described by Coypel in reminiscences which are worth quoting for their vivid picture of the studio battles of the past. '*Les disciples*,' he said, '*entrôient dans la querelle de leurs maîtres et foulôient aux pieds les ouvrages de ceux qu'ils croyôient opposés à leur sentiment; et l'on voyait distribuer des satyres qui, en attaquant le savoir des uns, déchirôient même jusqu'à leurs personnes. Dans cette guerre pittoresque, les uns arborâient l'étendard de Rubens, les autres celui de Poussin. Tandis que les partisans de Rubens accablôient le Poussin d'injures, les adorateurs de Poussin traitôient Rubens avec indignité. Mais quoique ces deux grands peintres fussent les seules divinités que l'on parassôit adorer, l'amour propre et l'envie faisôient tout agir. J'étais fort jeune alors, et ne connaissant point la malignité des cabales, comme je l'ai mieux connue depuis, je ne pouvôis comprendre comme on voulôit détruire une partie pour en faire valoir une autre.*'[9] The sketch is neat and Coypel succeeds in putting his finger on the essential fiction of the whole quarrel: that the two elements should really have been united, not in opposition.

The position, however, was not so much one of challenging the doctrines of the past, as of attempting to evolve a different point of view. Both sides to the dispute still agreed about various matters, and the ideal of drawing aimed at and practised by both of them was much the same. It was necessary, as Roger de Piles, the chief theorist of the opposition party, emphasized, for the student to follow all the elements which compose a drawing, such as anatomy and perspective. Drawing, he maintained, was the '*organe de nos pensées*'.[10] For this reason, it was necessary for the painter to have a deep knowledge of the antique. The two parties differed in the degree of their emphasis on drawing itself: to the Poussinistes, drawing alone was capable of depicting the '*choses réelles*' while colour could do no more than represent '*ce qui est accidentel*'. To the Rubenistes, on the contrary, colour was all important. Thenceforth painters were to derive inspiration not only from the Carraccis in the Palazzo Farnese but were to turn to the Rubens in the Luxembourg.

With Lebrun's death the tide-mark of the influence of the seventeenth century was reached: yet his teaching was to be remembered in the early years of the next century, and in 1721, for instance, Coypel spoke in praise of him before the Academy. Certain elements in his painting, such as the arabesque which was popularized by Vouet, were to reappear in the Rococo style proper, and his drawings with their directness and freshness were to compare with many of the eighteenth century. Signs of the Régence and of the Rococo were even to appear at Versailles. This change in taste was especially apparent in the architecture of Mansart whose Trianon dates from 1687 and in the sculpture of Girardon and Lepautre. Decoration evolved along those lines which were to culminate in the Rococo, the emergence of which was clearly indicated by the Dôme of the Invalides and the Chapel at Versailles. The Treaty of Ryswick concluded in 1698 allowed, moreover, a period of respite to the country, following the many defeats she had suffered in the past: and this recuperation enabled the arts to flourish.

Even Louis had responded to this new style, when, in discussions on the decorations for the apartments of the young Duchesse de Bourgogne, he stipulated that she must have works appropriate to her youth, a quality not apparent in the designs submitted to him. In a celebrated minute, he wrote: '*Il me paroit qu'il y a quelque chose à changer, que les sujets sont trop sérieux et qu'il faut qu'il y ait de la jeunesse mêlée dans ce que l'on fera. Vous m'apporterez des dessins quand vous viendrez, ou du moins des pensées. Il faut de l'enfance répandue partout.*'[11] The King was also much interested in the animal paintings of Desportes, and usually examined his preliminary drawings before the final version was painted. Desportes's success was significant and important: his paintings and drawings of animals have a directness unusual at this era; his drawing of the dogs which appear in his self-portrait in the Louvre (Pl. LIX) may have influenced Watteau. His landscapes, too, such as that in the Musée de Compiègne, show a different approach, that leads on to the naturalistic painting of Corot. Yet, at the same time, it would be wrong to over-emphasize the importance of the Rococo in these last years of the reign. The elements of a new style were present: the pastoral themes of the poets and painters, the Flemish inspiration, the reaction against Italy. But the time was not yet ripe for its complete emergence. The King's rejuvenation was only temporary. With the death of the Duchesse de Bourgogne in 1712, the court was plunged into gloom. 'The King,' wrote Madame de Maintenon, 'does everything he can to console himself but always falls into the same state of sadness. Everything is lacking, appears empty: there is no more joy, no more activity.' Only with the Regency was a measure of happiness to return to France.

NOTES TO CHAPTER I

[1] 'The sweetest moments are lost in immortalizing one's memory: Why seek glory so far afield? Pleasure is so close to us.'

[2] 'For this history, we have had to discover the new sources of Truth, to seek out our documents from newspapers, from pamphlets, from that whole world of dead and till now despised paper, from autographs, prints, drawings, pictures, and from all the intimate monuments which a period leaves behind it as its confession and resurrection.' *Histoire de la Société française pendant la Révolution* (édition définitive), Paris, 1929, p. vi.

[3] Maurice Fenaille in his *François Boucher*, 1925, p. 132, pointed out that a *Femme nue* by this artist was clearly apparent in a small painting by Ronmy of a dealer's stall on the corner of the Institut, which was in a Paris sale in 1923.

[4] William Sanderson, *Graphice. The Use of Pen and Pencil or The Most Excellent Art of Painting: in Two Parts*, London, 1658, p. 34.

[5] 'Man is said to be a sociable animal; on this account, it seems to me, no one is more of a man than a Frenchman; he is man *par excellence*, for he seems uniquely made for society.'

[6] 'It is not two or three drawings by Watteau, Boucher, Latour, that I must lend you. For what my brother and I have pursued with so much tenacity, and ferreted out with so much passion, is not this or that artist but a century, and the most essentially French century of our national

history.' Philip de Chennevières, 'Les Dessins des Maîtres anciens exposés à l'Ecole des Beaux-Arts', *Gazette des Beaux-Arts*, Vol. XX (1879), pp. 186–187.

[7] 'sober, pure and elevated manner'. Cited by Pierre Lavallée, 'Influences italiennes sur l'Evolution du Dessin français au XVIIe et au Début du XVIIIe Siècle' in: *Etudes italiennes*, Vol. V (1923), pp. 1–15.

[8] 'Monuments to their glory, expressing in a silent language their finest and most heroic actions.' Cited by Pierre Marcel, *La Peinture française au Début du XVIIIe Siècle* (1690–1725), Paris, 1913, p. 12.

[9] 'The disciples entered into the quarrel of their masters and trod underfoot the works of those whom they believed opposed to their opinions; satires were distributed which, while attacking men's knowledge, went as far as slanderously assaulting their persons. In this pictorial war, some raised the standard of Rubens, others that of Poussin. While the partisans of Rubens overwhelmed Poussin with obloquy, Poussin's adorers poured indignity on Rubens. But although these two great painters appeared to be the only divinities who were adored, in fact self esteem and envy were the real motives. I was very young at the time, and not knowing the malignity of intrigue, as I have since learnt to know it better, could not understand why people wished to destroy one party in order to enhance the reputation of another.' Antoine Coypel, *Discours prononcés dans les Conférences*, Paris, 1722, pp. 87, 88.

[10] *Cours de Peinture par Principe*, Paris, 1708, p. 127, cited by André Fontaine, *Les Doctrines d'Art en France*, Paris, 1909, p. 125.

[11] 'It appears to me that some things should be changed, that the subjects are too serious, and that there ought to be a certain youthfulness in what is undertaken. You will bring me some drawings when you come, or at least ideas. An air of youth must be diffused everywhere.' Written at Fontainebleau, 10 Septembre, 1699, cited by Fiske Kimball, *The Creation of the Rococo*, Philadelphia, 1943, p. 107.

II. THE REGENCY

AT VERSAILLES, the signs of the new style of painting had appeared only incidentally and as isolated elements. But elsewhere, in the circle of the Dauphin at Meudon, in that of the Duchesse de Maine at Sceaux and in that of the Duc d'Orléans at Paris and at Saint Cloud, other centres of artistic patronage existed which favoured a form of painting very different from that associated with the conventional art of the period. This style came to full fruition during the Regency that followed Louis XIV's death and which witnessed the transfer of the seat of government from Versailles to Paris. Under the Regency an immediate reaction occurred against the strict and sober morals of the last years of the former régime, and manifested itself in a widespread taste for dissipation. 'Les jeunes gens,' the Duchesse d'Orléans justly remarked, 'ne croient ni à Dieu ni à diable et regardent l'impiété et la dépravation comme une gentillesse.'[1] This general revolt against convention and desire for novelty was not to be without effect in painting.

The Regency was a moment of transition in French history, a watershed between two ways of living. A change was immediately apparent in the conduct of foreign affairs. The Regent, who was far from being a fool, did not attempt to pursue the grand aims of Louis XIV; on the contrary, he endeavoured to form an alliance with England against Spain and secure for the country the tranquillity that was so necessary if the defeats of the previous régime were to be redeemed. His policy, Michelet shrewdly observed, was a sign of the new age, a symbol of modernity as opposed to reaction, represented by the antiquated and dying Imperialism of Spain. Unfortunately, the Regent's aims were hampered by chronic financial disorder and, above all, by the failure of the ambitious plans for economic development and for colonial expansion floated by the Scottish financier and adventurer, John Law. The losses suffered by private individuals in the crash of the Law Bank were severe, the disillusionment widespread. Many artists such as Gillot and Largillière were ruined, and the nervous line and satirical touch of this period may perhaps be a result of the insecurity engendered by an inflation and comparable to the art which flourished in Germany after the 1914–1918 war.

Yet, despite the dissipation that is so often and so rightly associated with the Regent's name and reign, these transitional years between the two centuries were rich in artistic achievement. They witnessed the appearance of the greatest painter of the eighteenth century, Antoine Watteau, and of a more appreciative public for the fine arts. The Regent himself led the way in the general feeling for an art that was modern and capable of expressing the tendencies of the moment. A connoisseur and amateur artist, he characteristically took the subject for a series of book illustrations and for the decoration of one of his private apartments at Meudon from the fables of Daphnis et Chloë, a choice which reflected the growing predilection for pastoralism that had found so exquisite an expression in La Fontaine's Fables. In addition, he bought fine paintings in Italy through

11

the agency of the banker Crozat, and commissioned Antoine Coypel to paint a series of fourteen decorations, representing 'The History of Aeneas', for the Grand Galleries in the Palais Royal (1702). He was always open to new ideas, always ready to meet artists. Rosalba Carriera, for instance, during her visit to Paris to see her brother-in-law, A. Pellegrini, who was engaged on a series of frescos for the Law Bank, recorded in her diary her encounter with the Regent and his mistress, Madame de Parabère.

Paris had now become the artistic as well as the political centre of France. The gay and convivial atmosphere was greatly stimulated by the balls held at the Opéra and in the Tuileries, by the liveliness of the theatre and by the return of the Commedia dell'Arte led by the celebrated Riccoboni. In this moment of general freedom and expansion, many new buildings appeared in the capital. The needs of their interior decoration, in which the mirror played a large part, helped to popularize the cabinet or *genre* painting and to create a new style. The patrons of the Regency, whether they came from the old nobility, who were beginning to reside in Paris, or from the ranks of the *nouveaux riches*, demanded a different sort of painting from that of the old régime: they required, not coldly classical or allegorical compositions, but charming and gaily coloured paintings to enliven their apartments and form an appropriate setting for the elegant *soupers* of the era. The consequences of this change in taste were profound: they were neatly analysed much later by the architect, Patte, writing in 1760. '*Ce changement dans nos intérieurs,*' he said, '*fit aussi substituer à la gravité des ornements dont on les surchargeait, toutes sortes de décorations de menuiserie, légères, pleines de goût, variées de mille façons diverses. On supprima les solives apparentes des planchers et on les revêtit de ces plafonds qui donnent tant de grâce aux appartements et que l'on décore de frises et de toutes sortes d'ornements agréables; au lieu de ces tableaux ou de ces énormes bas-reliefs que l'on plaçait sur les cheminées, on les a décorées de glaces qui, par leur répétition avec celles qu'on leur oppose, forment des tableaux mouvants qui grandissent et animent les appartements, et leur donnent un air de gaîté et de magnificence qu'ils n'avaient pas.*'[2] The practical needs of the moment, no less than the spirit of the times, pointed in the direction of a new and gracious style.

Colour began to bloom again in French painting. It was led in by a two-fold action, firstly by the example of Flemish painters, such as Van der Meulen or Genoëls, who were resident in France, and, secondly, by the visits of French painters to the Low Countries and to England. The carefully formulated views of one such traveller, Largillière, for instance, who devoted much attention to the place of colour in composition, were carefully remembered and passed on by Oudry, who had worked in his studio. Largillière's own portraits are in complete contrast to those of his immediate predecessors. His groups of rich Paris merchants and bourgeois, which are now known mainly from oil sketches, show him to have been primarily interested in the dramatic possibilities of a theme related by colour and composition. His paintings contain much of the exciting tempo of the period. This new note is clearly apparent in the brilliant portrait of himself, his wife and his daughter (Paris, Louvre). The figures are seen against a landscape background; the decorative possibilities of their costume and the charm of the women is accentuated. His delicious

12

portrait of *Mlle Duclos* (Chantilly, Musée Condé), for instance, abounds in theatricality. She is painted as a woman, vivid and real, not as a myth. It is already an indication of the way in which painting and the stage were to be so closely connected during the century; as Coypel neatly declared in a lecture given before the Académie royale de peinture in 1721, '*Tout contribue dans les spectacles à l'instruction du peintre, les idées, les images et les passions, exprimées par la poésie, et par les gestes des grands acteurs, les postures, les attitudes, la noblesse et la grâce du ballet et des danseurs.*'[3] This was an approach that appeared even at the very end of the century, when Neo-Classicism was in power, in David's *Marat assassiné* (Musée de Versailles), in which the scene is rendered with a forceful realism that has the pungency of a dramatic passage.

In the early years of the century, indeed, a portraitist such as Rigaud, who still worked within the conventions of the seventeenth century, excelling in the formal dignified portrait, did not hesitate to paint a provincial magistrate, Gaspard de Gueidan, as a theatrical figure (Musée d'Aix). The direct representation of theatrical performances was to become a frequent occurrence in eighteenth-century painting, and was to persist down to the Revolution. Antoine Coypel, for instance, treated the *Evanouissement d'Esther devant Assuérus* (Louvre) with all the drama the incident required; but he did more: in his rich and sombre colouring, in his decorative manner of painting, and in his dramatic ability, he revealed that the lessons of the Flemish school had been digested. He was already in accord with the spirit of the new age. His histrionic touch was as typical of the Regency as Santerre's erotic depiction of *Suzanne* (Louvre). A similar lightness of effect can be perceived in the drawing of this generation, in Largillière's portrait of the *Dauphin as a Boy* (New York, Mrs Stralem) with its memories of Lely and Van Dyck, or in Coypel's sketch of a boy in the Louvre which both recalls Rubens and anticipates Watteau.

Flemish painters, of course, had long been settled in Paris, living mainly in the quarter of Saint Germain des Près. They formed a closed and influential colony; and a measure of their assimilation in the artistic life of the country can be seen in the appointment of Nicholas Wleughels to the post of Director of the French Academy at Rome, an office not without diplomatic responsibilities. Flemish and Dutch paintings had long been available in Paris: they could be found in the markets, while works by the more important masters were in the notable collections of the period. The charming and cultivated Madame de Verrue had a number of paintings by Rubens and Van Dyck, by Metsu and Dou in her collection, as well as works by such modern artists as Chardin, Lancret and Pater. She was the former mistress of the King of Savoy; her house on the corner of the rue du Cherche Midi and the rue du Régent was the meeting place for a small and select group of amateurs, which included Louis XIV's natural daughter, Mlle de Nantes, and her lover the Comte de Lassay, also a collector, and two relatives of Jean de Jullienne, de Glucq and de Montullé. Her salon was to be typical of many of the period: she continued the tradition of the *Précieuses*, but the atmosphere was less pedantic and livelier. Her collection was one of many which contained important paintings from the Low Countries.

13

Even Rembrandt, who might seem at first sight so opposed to the taste of the period, had his devoted followers. Rigaud had seven of his paintings in his collection; Santerre, Raoux and Grimou followed him; and even an artist such as Bernard Picart, who is generally connected with the *fête galante*, copied his drawings.[4]

Picart himself was one of the leaders of the movement away from formal painting towards the gayer and more elegant style of the Regency. It was a movement which, until the emergence of Watteau, appeared almost exclusively in drawings and engravings. Modern artists began to find their themes in the theatre, in literature and in the ordinary occurrences of everyday life. They found rich and rewarding sources in gallantry and in the relations between the sexes. Picart and Simpol were clearly precursors of Watteau and the style of the *fête galante*. No direct borrowing by Watteau from Simpol can be traced but, as Madame Adhémar has shown,[5] certain means of approach and methods of treatment are common to both. Simpol's engraving of *Le cavalier achetant des dentelles*, for instance, treats the same sort of theme in the same sort of manner as Watteau's painting *L'Enseigne de Gersaint* (Potsdam, Sans Souci); Picart's print *L'Ouïe*, on the other hand, recalls the pose of the lovers in the *Embarquement pour Cythère* (Louvre, and Potsdam, Sans Souci). What is so interesting is to see how already Picart in his charming sketch of *Pelerins de l'Isle de Cythère*, representing the Regent and Mlle Desmares (Victoria and Albert Museum), was treating the same sort of theme as Watteau; the source for their whole conception moreover was derived from a contemporary play, Dancourt's *Les Trois Cousines*. Thus, during these important formative years, conditions were prepared for the artist who alone could combine all these scattered elements in a coherent style, itself the outcome of a positive and personal attitude to life.

Of all the artists at work during this transitional period, none, perhaps, both incorporated the characteristics of the new style and played so large a part in effecting their transmission as Claude Gillot. He was an artist of small talent, but much personality. His few known paintings reveal no particular ability: one of his better works, the *Deux Carosses* (Louvre), is hard and wooden in composition and dull in colour. He made his mark essentially as a draughtsman. Here he brought to his work an eye for the contemporary scene, a journalist's ability to catch the amusing and piquant aspects of life. His vivid and fresh notation of events makes him the ancestor of Daumier and Toulouse-Lautrec. His self-portrait reveals a man of humorous disposition: his quizzical face is alive with wit and fun. His subjects and his manner sound a new note. This *dernier païen*, as the Brothers Goncourt termed him, found excitement and satisfaction in drawing the Bacchanalian feasts and the scenes of nymphs and satyrs to which his thin spidery line gave a new and uncommon edge.

He liked, as his subject, anything which was out of the ordinary, or surprising and modern in feeling. He found his chief inspiration in the world of the theatre, especially in the fascinating and gay antics of the *Commedia dell' Arte*. This form of entertainment was long established in France, though in 1697, for an alleged slight on Madame de Maintenon, the troupe at the Hôtel de Bourgogne had been expelled from Paris. Gillot,

14

though not the first artist to have taken his themes from its effervescent humour, was the first to endow its reproduction in visual form with the drollery of the original. His spirited drawing of the *Mort de Maître André*, one of a series in the Louvre, presents the very essence of the *Commedia* (Pl. LXI). He designed scenery and costumes for the Opéra, but he was essentially a spectator, the recorder of what went on during the actual performance. He saw the play in action and, as in a pair of drawings in the British Museum and in an English private collection, noted down the histrionic effects of the celebrated Baron, the greatest actor of his day, playing in Corneille and Racine.

Though these two notations of the legitimate stage are brilliant in their impressionistic suggestion of movement, Gillot was at his best in his drawings of the *Commedia dell' Arte*. So devoted was he to this amusement that, when the *Commedia dell' Arte* proper was exiled from Paris, he regularly attended the less polished and more primitive versions performed in the fairs on the outskirts of the city, and even wrote several scenarios for them. An appreciator of life, he was able to convey wit and fun by means of line. His work was varied and unequal (the drawings for the *Passion de Jésus Christ* in the Bibliothèque Royale at Brussels are pedestrian in the extreme) but will always continue to fascinate. His theatrical drawings, his arabesques (many of which were engraved by Huquier or by Gillot himself) and his illustrations for La Motte's *Fables* (Chantilly, Musée Condé) formed an important link between the draughtsmanship of Callot and Bellange and that of the eighteenth century. Besides all else his importance is assured for posterity as the master of Watteau. He turned Watteau towards the theatre, enabled him to liberate his personal idiom and paved the way for the emergence of the elegance and wit, the grace and refinement of the Régence style.

Antoine Watteau dominates the first half of the eighteenth century, the epitome of its charm, the master of the Regency. He is the supreme draughtsman of the period, the poignant and sensitive spirit of whose art has been analysed so exactly and so correctly by the Goncourts in their celebrated essay. He appeared on the scene at the very moment he was needed. Reaching the maturity of his style when the various conflicting tendencies of the early eighteenth century required some form of synthesis, he was able to fuse all these scattered elements into his own painting. In his work can be discovered not only elements from the past, the arabesque, the incipient, fumbling attempts to evolve the *fête galante* style and the use of a richer and more poetical artistic instrument, but those of the future, a love of nature, a passionate interest in all types of society, and an impressionistic technique. He was himself the product of a synthesis. By origin Flemish, his first paintings, notably the *Danse* (St Petersburg, Hermitage), clearly demonstrate an early dependence on Teniers. Yet, how quickly his style and content changed once he was in France: immediately and irrevocably he became a Parisian. After several years of hack-work, he entered the studio of Gillot, who confirmed him in his love of drawing from the life. His eyes were opened to all sorts of exciting and fascinating themes. He learnt much from Gillot, as can be seen in the similarities between Gillot's line and his own early drawings, but their temperaments, no less than their tastes, were too similar

15

for them to remain together for long: they quarrelled and parted. But from his years with Gillot he retained that love of drawing strange types and of building up a repertoire of curious or straightforward scenes which he was to put to such effective use in his paintings.

The period of training under Claude II Audran that followed introduced him to a different circle of artists and to a new range of experience. With Audran, he joined the tradition of the 'ornamentalists', the tradition of Brebiette and Bérain. Audran himself had taken the lead in executing those painted decorations of surface which, at Anet and, above all, in the Château de la Ménagerie (where he collaborated with Antoine Coypel), had prepared the way for the emergence of the Régence style and of the Rococo itself. It was at Meudon, for instance, that Audran painted his *Berceau où les singes sont à table* which was to inaugurate that characteristic style of 'singeries', grotesques and ornamentation which was so typical of the century as a whole. How deeply Watteau, who worked with Audran in the years 1708 and 1709, was involved in the preparation or execution of designs for the Château is not quite clear. What, at any rate, is certain is that much of his own work, his paintings as well as his purely ornamental designs, owes its inspiration to the example of Audran and his collaborators at Meudon, Louis de Boullogne and François Desportes.

Audran was not only an interior decorator, he was *concierge* or keeper of the Luxembourg, which then housed Rubens's *Vie de Marie de Médicis*. During his stay with Audran at the Luxembourg, Watteau deepened his appreciation of nature, drawing those clumps of trees that were to be found in its gardens, and studied intently Rubens's superb paintings; these works, whether through engravings (for which Charles Natoire executed a series of red chalk drawings in 1708–1710), or from personal visits, were to form one of the most vital influences on eighteenth-century art. The contrast between Rubens and Watteau was distinct: the one, rich in physical vigour, energetic, and in touch with life in all its phases; the other, delicate, melancholy, yet charged with a febrile, intense energy derived perhaps from his consumption. But it was in the exuberant drama of Rubens that he found much to aid his own art. The degree of his dependence on Rubens is well known; it is exactly illustrated in Watteau's *Sleeping Nymph* (Louvre), in his drawings, and in so original and brilliant a painting as the *Embarquement pour Cythère*, where whole passages, such as the *amoretti* curling round the masts of the ship, are derived from Rubens. From Rubens, too, he learnt much in the way of handling his paint. Though the origins of the *fête galante* as a theme lie in Poussin, Bourdon and his more immediate predecessors Picart and Simpol, or in the Venetians, it was essentially Rubens's example in the superb *Garden of Love* (Dresden Gallery) that enabled him to find the expression of his genius in this so congenial subject.

Watteau, indeed, was one of those artists whose imagination was fired by the stimulus of contact with the work of other painters. Yet there is no question of plagiarism or even of weakness of conception; he simply digested elements from the works of other masters and fused them with his own contribution to form the finished picture. But he always felt

16

the need to confirm his own viewpoint by contact with other artists. Soon after leaving Audran, he went to live in the mansion of the banker Crozat, one of the richest men in Paris—not because he considered such a patron's support useful but because of his magnificent collection of drawings. '*L'occasion favorable qu'il eut ensuite d'entrer chez M. de Crozat lui convint d'autant mieux*,' Gersaint declared, '*qu'il scavoit les grands trésors en desseins que possêdoit ce curieux, il en profita avec avidité, et il ne connoissoit d'autres plaisirs que celui d'examiner continuellement, et même de copier tous les morceaux des plus grands maîtres.*'[6] Crozat's collection was, in fact, one of the most splendid of an age that was rich in private collections. It contained not only some four hundred paintings and pieces of sculpture but some nineteen thousand drawings. These included an impressive selection of works by Rubens and by Venetian masters, some of which were duly reproduced in the *Recueil d'Estampes d'après les tableaux du Cabinet du Roi, de duc d'Orléans et d'autres cabinets*. Crozat was a sympathetic character, as well as a munificent patron. His house was the scene of concerts that were described by Rosalba Carriera and attended by Watteau, who may even have left a record of the musicians. He was not one of those collectors who preserved their collections in strict secrecy. His doors were always open to amateurs and artists. '*M. Crozat*,' Mariette wrote after Watteau's death, '*n'aimait point ses dessins pour lui seul; il se faisait, au contraire, un plaisir de les faire voire aux amateurs, toutes les fois qu'ils le lui demandaient, et il ne refusait pas même d'en aider les artistes. On tenait assez régulièrement toutes les semaines des assemblées chez lui, où j'ai eu pendant longtemps, le bonheur de me trouver; et c'est autant aux ouvrages des grands maîtres, qu'on y considérait, qu'aux entretiens des habiles gens qui s'y réunissaient, que je dois le peu des connoissances que j'ai acquises.*'[7]

In Crozat's house, Watteau was able to study the art of the Venetians and to understand those secrets of evoking colour and atmosphere which they had made their own. The influence of their rich and sumptuous art appears in many of his works, in his *Antiope* (Louvre) or in *L'Amour desarmé* (Chantilly, Musée Condé), which is directly inspired by a Venetian drawing once in Crozat's collection and now in the Louvre. His many copies after drawings by masters of this school include free and attractive sketches after Titian, Campagnola and Baroccio. His attentive understanding of the Venetians helped to enrich the responsiveness of his own temperament and formed the sources for many of his masterpieces, the *Fêtes Vénétiennes* (Edinburgh, National Gallery) and *The Ball* (Dulwich), which owe so much of their inspiration to the warm and humanistic art of Venice.

The most superlative draughtsman of his age, Watteau, in his short lifetime, produced a rich and varied selection of drawings, of which over six hundred are now known. He was excellent both in his choice of subject—his taste was exquisite—and in the singular felicity of his medium. He almost invariably chose, as Dr K. T. Parker has pointed out in his authoritative volume,[8] a red chalk, which is usually of a rich crimson colour, distinguishable from the yellow shade of the previous century. His superb use of chalk, his beloved sanguine, enabled him to give his drawings their plasticity of effect and deepness of colour;

on occasion, to heighten his effects, he would use red chalk subordinate to black chalk and, at others, black chalk and pencil to the exclusion of sanguine. To reach his most highly charged combinations of colour, he would at times employ what was virtually a technique of *quatre crayons*, two shades of red chalk combined with white and black. His use of pastel was rarer and he is known, from an entry in the sale catalogue of Jean de Jullienne, to have worked in gouache. Pen he employed on occasions but, as D'Argenville pointed out, this was the only linear medium in which he did not excel.[9]

What is always so impressive about Watteau's drawing is the spontaneity, the effortless manner in which he catches the essence of a theme without loss of directness. His drawings show no hesitation, no lack of certainty. He drew immediately and with complete satisfaction: his drawings reflect his own pleasure in creation. He rarely considered drawing as a means of directly preparing for a picture, and the only drawing known as a fully worked-up study for a painting is the full-length nude in the Groult collection which served for his painting *La Remède* in a Paris private collection. In his delicious red chalk drawing of *Moïse sauvé des Eaux* (Pl. X), however, is a suggestion of the same delicate manner in which he could form a compositional drawing. On the contrary, Watteau's method was to draw first and then turn to his drawings when he wished to paint a picture. In his celebrated lecture to the Académie Royale de Peinture, in 1748, the Comte de Caylus revealed that it had been Watteau's custom to preserve his drawings in a bound volume. '*Quand il lui prenoit en gré de faire un tableau il avoit recours à son recueil. Il y choisissoit les figures qui lui convenoient le mieux pour le moment. Il en formoit ses groupes, le plus souvent en conséquence d'un fonds de paysage qu'il avoit conçu ou préparé.*'[10]

In these drawings, Watteau was essentially a realist: he recorded the objects and the faces of the tangible world surrounding him. Paradoxically, when he turned to paint, these fragments of reality were subordinated to a vision which was imaginative and poetic. In the heat of his creation, those figures, Wleughels, Sirois the dealer, Mlle Dangeville the actress, the dogs he borrowed from Testa, and the cupids derived from Rubens, were transmuted into the inhabitants of a dreamlike world. They have no connection with tangible existence: their world is untrammelled by the pre-occupations of daily life: time is suspended and only on occasion is allowed to disturb their moments of exquisite enjoyment. All the dreams and longings which Honoré d'Urfé had described in his voluminous novel *L'Astrée*, all the figures that surrounded him in daily life, are metamorphosed in the creation of a land of fairy palaces and silvery trees.

Those delicate female faces with their mocking eyes, their ever-changing smiles, those faces that beckon us but which we can never identify, move from the realm of the known to the middle distances of the *Champs Elysées*, the *Charmes de la Vie*, and the *Embarquement pour Cythère*. With their silken dresses, their delicious provocative coiffures, their glitter and their charm, they are the eternal 'pélérines', for ever on the point of departure for the Isles of Cythère, and the fulfilment of their dreams.

The curtain is lifted on a world bathed in mellow golden sunlight, on pillars that enclose an enchanted island. The water splashes gently from a fountain, the strings of the mandoline sound their captivating 'chansons'. Pierrot and Columbine pass across the stage, to be followed by the lonely forgotten face of Gilles, the tragic clown. It is the quintessence of civilization, a fragile world permeated always by a hint of melancholy, a note of questioning. But though life may contain its tragedies, its uncertainties, though it may and must mean that possession of love is never complete, always transitory, yet even in the knowledge that the experience of the moment is only partial there lies a solution, something of the eternal. It is the conscious, rational apprehension that pleasure without limitation would prove stale; that the very transitoriness of pleasure is the measure of its eternal value for the individual.

'*Quand partons-nous pour le Bonheur?*' asked Baudelaire. It is Watteau's quest. All is transitory, all may melt, yet in the contemplation of the visual splendours of existence lies consolation. He is the painter of melancholy, but also of love; his art remains for all time the symbol of happiness. He has distilled into the crisp lines of his drawings, the breathing forms of his hands, the fresh carnations of his paint, the intensity of life itself. For all his absorption in the definition of pleasure, in the creation of an imaginary world, he never forgot that the basis of his art was its reality; and in one of his finest and last works, the *Enseigne de Gersaint*, he created a masterpiece of realism.

Watteau's success amongst the amateurs of Paris was immediate. His paintings and drawings were eagerly disputed by an appreciative circle of collectors, so that, by twenty years after his death, the King of Prussia's envoy, the Count de Rothenburg, was compelled to inform his master that '*J'ai milles peines à trouver des tableaux de Watteau qui sont d'une rareté extrême.*'[11] They had, he pointed out, nearly all crossed the Channel to English collections, where, indeed, they were to be found in those of Dr Mead and Sir Joshua Reynolds. The immediacy of Watteau's triumph is striking: for despite its origins in the prints of Picart and Simpol, his art was essentially a modern production. No less striking was the way in which his drawings were cherished. '*Pour ses desseins, quand ils sont de son bon temps, c'est-à-dire depuis qu'il est sorti de chez M. de Crozat,*' wrote one of his contemporaries, Gersaint',[12] '*rien n'est au dessus dans ce genre; la finesse, les grâces, la légèreté, la correction, la facilité, l'expression, enfin on n'y désire rien, et il passera toujours pour un des plus grands et un des meilleurs dessinateurs que la France ait donnés.*'

It was hardly surprising, then, that, soon after his premature death, the charming Jean de Jullienne, the *administrateur* of the Gobelins factory and one of Watteau's closest friends, began the publication of a series of volumes reproducing his works. Characteristically, he opened the series with the *Figures de differents Caractères, de Paysages et d'Etudes*, which appeared in two handsome folio volumes in 1726–1728, and contained three hundred and fifty-one etchings after his drawings, as well as a short biography of him. These valuable volumes are of great importance in identifying Watteau's drawings, although Jean de Jullienne sometimes etched on separate pages drawings which in fact were on the same sheet. This publication was followed in 1735 by the *Oeuvre gravé de*

Watteau; some of the finest engravers of the period collaborated in this book which mainly contained paintings, though a few drawings were included in it.

Watteau's manner could be adopted and imitated, but not the unique quality of his spirit. His followers were numerous; their work, though possessing skill and charm, is essentially that of *petits maîtres*. Clever and competent though they are, they lack the subtlety and refinement which was the gift of the master. As a painter, Pater is fresh in colour and his sense of composition is considerable; he had, too, invention in his choice of subject matter. Though his drawings are pleasing and delicate (Pl. XXVIII) they have not the quality of Lancret. For Lancret, a lover of the theatre, a connoisseur of painting, had a flair for subjects, a sensibility which enabled him to respond with immediacy and precision; his exquisite sheets of studies of female heads or male figures have some of those crisp and fresh qualities which distinguish Watteau's draughtsmanship. He had, too, the ability to infuse his drawings with a gusto that is rarely found in the artists of Watteau's entourage: his study for the laughing man in the *Déjeuner au Jambon* is a brilliant essay in characterization (Pl. LI).

The modernity of Watteau's style exerted an immediate appeal throughout Europe. His disciples travelled throughout the continent, to England, to Spain and Portugal, to Poland and to Germany. Their painting had his charm, though often it barely rose above the second rate. Perhaps one of the most accomplished was Pesne, who lived for long in Germany: his portraiture was vigorous and well observed and in his drawings (Berlin, Print Room) he could suggest at times the poetry and fantasy of the *fête galante*. To England, Mercier carried much of the Régence spirit, and his conversation pictures, such as those belonging to Lord Rothermere and Lord Brownlow, did much to introduce a decorative note into English painting. Watteau's influence was to be seen, indeed, in Hogarth, Nollekens, Gainsborough and, later, in Stothard. The same gracious elements of composition appeared in Mercier's rare drawings, such as those in the Cotton collection, Plymouth, and in Mr J. N. Bryson's possession at Oxford (Pl. XXVII). But of all the minor artists working within the Watteau convention, Chantereau was best able to suggest something of the master's ability: his silken, delicate *Festival* (Louvre) or his sketch of a small boy at Stockholm (Pl. XXI) possess a freshness and personality that is altogether missing from the work of other followers such as Octavien, Angillis and de Bar.

Another group of artists also turned to certain elements within Watteau's art; the decorators and ornamentalists, who developed the Régence style into that of the Rococo, had various points of contact with the *fête galante*. Lajoue, for instance, invested his curving forms with something of the grace of the master (Pl. XXXV). Yet with them, the restraint of the Régence disappeared; their drawings for arabesques and for ornaments were rich in luxuriant and extreme forms, in scrolls and curves, of which the most fantastic examples occurred in Meissonier's *Livre nouveau de divers morceaux de fantaisie*, published at the very end of the Rococo movement in 1745. They digested and made their own, and played endless variations on those *Chinoiseries* and *singeries* which Watteau himself had used in some of his ornamental drawings. Yet for all its over-exuberance, the art of Pineau, Oppenord, Lajoue and Meissonier had a genuine spark of creation. They possessed the positive and brilliant spirit of the Régence and the Rococo, which in its most measured and gracious moments, its most poignant and intellectual aspects, had found its highest expression in Watteau.

NOTES TO CHAPTER II

[1] 'The younger generation believes neither in God nor in the devil, and regards impiety and depravity as social graces.'

[2] 'This change in the interiors of our houses meant also that in place of the solemn ornaments with which they were overloaded, all kinds of decorations in wood-work have been substituted, light, tasteful and varied in a thousand different ways. The visible joists in the roofs made way for those ceilings which give such an air of grace to apartments, and are decorated with friezes and all sorts of agreeable ornaments; instead of those pictures and huge bas-reliefs which used to be placed on the mantelpieces, they have been decorated with numerous mirrors which, as they reflect each other, compose moving pictures that enlarge and animate the apartments, and give them an air of gaiety and magnificence which they did not have before.' Cited by Louis Gillet: *Histoire des Arts* (*Histoire de la Nation française*. Ed. G. Hanotaux. Paris, 2 vols., 1922. Vol. 2, p. 383).

[3] 'Everything on the stage helps to instruct the painter: the ideas, images and passions expressed by poetry and by the gestures of great actors, the positions, attitudes, nobility and the grace of the ballet and of the dancers.' *Discours prononcés dans les Conférences de l'Académie Royale*. Paris, 1771, cited by André Blum: 'La Mode des Portraits Mythologiques en France sous Louis XV' in *La Revue du dix-huitième Siècle*, Vol. I, No. 3 (1913), p. 308.

[4] Lot 162 of the William Bateson Sale, London, Messrs Sotheby & Co., 23-24 April, 1929, included a red chalk signed drawing by Picart after Rembrandt's *Cimon and Pero*.

[5] 'Sources de l'Art de Watteau: Claude Simpol' in *Prométhée* (*L'Amour de l'Art*: Nouvelle Série), Vol. III (1939), pp. 67–74.

[6] 'The favourable opportunity of entering M. Crozat's household, which subsequently came his way, suited him all the better since he knew of the magnificent collection of drawings which this connoisseur possessed. He took advantage of it avidly, and his greatest pleasure was to examine continually, and even to copy, the pieces of the greatest masters.' *Catalogue de Feu M. de Lorangère* par E. F. Gersaint, Paris, 1744, No. 94, p. 170, reprinted by Pierre Champion, *Notes Critiques sur Les Vies anciennes d'Antoine Watteau*, Paris, 1921, p. 59.

[7] 'It was not for himself alone that M. Crozat loved his drawings; on the contrary, he enjoyed showing them to collectors whenever they asked him, he even allowed artists to profit by them. Reunions took place regularly every week at his house, where for a long time I have had the pleasure of being present; and it is as much to the works of the great masters who were examined there, as to the conversation of the clever people who met there, that I owe what little knowledge I have acquired.' *Description sommaire des Dessins de grands Maîtres du Cabinet de Feu M. Crozat*, Paris, 1741, p. ix.

[8] *The Drawings of Antoine Watteau*, London, 1932.

[9] K. T. Parker, 'Sidelights on Antoine Watteau', *Old Master Drawings*, Vol. X (1935), pp. 3–9.

[10] 'When he wished to paint a picture he had recourse to his collection. He chose there the figures which suited him best for the moment. With these he composed his groups, most often in accordance with a background of landscape which he had conceived or prepared.' 'La Vie d'Antoine Watteau . . . lue à l'Académie Royale . . . le 3 février, 1743.' P. Champion: *op. cit.*, p. 101.

[11] 'I have the greatest difficulty in finding Watteau's pictures which are extremely rare.' Cited by R. Rey: *Quelques Satellites de Watteau*, Paris, 1931, p. 21.

[12] 'As for his drawings, when they are of his good period, that is, since he left M. Crozat's house, they are unsurpassed. He has finesse, grace, lightness, correctness, ease and power of expression—in a word, nothing is lacking, and he will always rank as one of the greatest and best draughtsmen that France has produced.' P. Champion: *op. cit.*, p. 65.

ANTOINE WATTEAU: A Woman at her Toilet

III. TRIUMPH OF THE ROCOCO

THE REGENCY had effected a revolution in the forms of French art and in the conditions of life. The gaiety and vivacity of the Regent's circle at the Palais Royal were to impart a character to the age as a whole. Despite the fluctuations of policy, at home and abroad, the middle years of the eighteenth century were happy ones for France. Such wars as took place, the Wars of the Polish Succession, and the Austrian Succession, and the Seven Years War, were all on foreign soil. France's defeats were certainly heavy; but even the loss to Britain of such rich fields for colonial expansion and potential sources of wealth as Canada and India had little effect on French public opinion. Society was contented and happy with the many delights of Parisian life. Having no particular preoccupation with international problems, and generally no financial worries, its members could devote themselves to the study of art, the fascinations of philosophy, and the pleasures of abstract discussion. Life was comfortable and, as the country increased in prosperity, the middle class emerged as a powerful political and cultural force in national life.

The arts and crafts reflected this rise in the standard of living. It was an age that produced some of the finest furniture, the most exquisitely designed stuffs, the most beautifully worked silver, and the most delicate porcelain in Europe. Never, indeed, have the domestic arts achieved such grace and distinction as they did in eighteenth-century France, when even the domestic utensils used by the middle class or the poorer people reflected this desire to possess objects of taste. A painting, such as Boucher's *Le Déjeuner* (Louvre) suggests, as Monsieur Verlet has aptly remarked,[1] the characteristic atmosphere of the interiors of the period, with its table of red and black lacquer, its silver coffee pot, and its cups of Meissen and Chantilly ware.

That a French interior should possess objects from other countries and from overseas was typical of the period. Expansion was in the air. France not only gave much to Europe; she was herself open to all sorts of extraneous influences. Yet though she derived many of her philosophical ideas from England and for certain of her artistic conceptions turned to the East, she fused such outside elements into a conception of her own. The keynotes of the period were diffusion and criticism: every aspect of human activity had to be tested and questioned. '*Chaque siècle*,' wrote Diderot to the Princess Dashkoff in 1771, '*a son esprit qui le caractèrise. L'esprit de notre siècle est celui de la liberté.*'[2] In politics, in ideas, in literature and in art, the tendency was increasingly one of revolt against authority, against the Church and finally against the Crown itself. Together with the general current of scepticism ran a preoccupation with man as the measure of all things: the lessons of Pope and of Locke were not forgotten by French men of letters and thinkers. The aim of the *Philosophes* was clear and startling: to break down the barriers which seemed to exist against the expansion of knowledge. For all its apparent frivolity, for all its love of pleasure, the eighteenth century was essentially a serious age. The Salons resounded with discussion; and the topics debated in Paris were eagerly followed in the courts of Germany and Russia.

These tendencies were apparent in art as well as in life. Art was directed to the service of society, not only to that of the court. The status of the Crown itself had changed. The Monarchy was absolute, but its foundations were no longer so sure. Louis XV was not an autocrat like his great-grandfather. He had, it is true, inherited the traditional constitution of his family and was physically strong, but his powers of application were weak. A martyr to *ennui*, he desired distraction at any price; as the Duc d'Antin observed, *il ne sentira rien*. He was industrious, but little more. He had moments of insight, as when he saw that France's policy lay in support for Austria rather than Prussia, and when he adopted a firm attitude to the *Parlement*. But on the whole, he was content to follow the advice first of Cardinal Fleury and later of the Duc de Choiseul and of Madame de Pompadour. Bored by the duties of his office, he sought above all to escape from the formalities of court life. Anxious for comfort and sympathy, once the shortlived charms of Marie Lecinska had passed, he found solace in the arms of his mistresses, with Mesdames de Mailly, de Pompadour and Dubarry. The famous *petits cabinets*, his rural retreats and his Châteaux were his *îles de Cythère*.

Louis's patronage of contemporary art was necessarily considerable. His taste was decided, though he had never the potent influence on style that had so distinguished Louis XIV. He clearly cared for works of art. On the walls of his bedroom were to be found paintings by Rubens, Van Dyck, Poussin, Raphael, Holbein and Titian. In his dining-room, he could see Lancret's *Déjeuner de Jambon* and J. F. de Troy's *Déjeuner d'huîtres* (Chantilly, Musée Condé). The galleries to his apartments celebrated his liking for the chase and were hung with *chasses exotiques* by Boucher, de Troy, Carle van Loo, Parrocel and Pater. With his love of hunting and outdoor life, he was naturally interested in the work of J. B. Oudry. For his sculpture he turned to J. B. Lemoyne.

Keenly interested in architecture, he appointed Gabriel to be his *premier architecte* and entrusted him with the building of the apartments of the Queen and the Dauphin at Versailles. Gabriel also enlarged the King's own rooms: in doing so he had to demolish the splendid *escalier des Ambassadeurs*. He also undertook other commissions at Fontainebleau and at Choisy. Besides the actual construction of the building, all problems relating to interior decoration fascinated him. Louis XV is said always to have looked at, and at times even to have corrected the design of models of the most important pieces of furniture submitted for his approval, and to have personally inspected all the pieces of furniture or *objets d'art* destined as presents. On occasion, too, he bought works of art in the Paris sale rooms, where a right of pre-emption was exercised in his favour. His taste for fine objects and furniture was shared by the Queen. Though her funds were limited, she always took a decided part in any scheme for redecorating her rooms and, like the King, would usually comment on the preliminary sketches and designs. She was also an eager, if not particularly talented, amateur artist, and was taught by Oudry.

Though Louis XV's patronage of the arts was of a private rather than a public nature, the structure of the artistic administration in France remained much the same as it had been under Louis XIV. The encouragement of the arts depended on the *Directeur-Général des Bâtiments du Roi*, who frequently leant heavily for advice on the *Premier Peintre*. The extent of the commands lavished on artists depended greatly on the personality of the *Directeur* and the extent to which he could be influenced by the *Premier Peintre* and the Academy. For despite the opposition of the Académie de Saint Luc and the attempts to overthrow its supremacy, the Académie Royale de Peinture remained the principal centre of art; nearly every important artist of the period had studied in it.[3] It was from the *Directeur-Général*, again, that orders were issued to the various agencies dependent on the Crown, the Académie de France at Rome (the correspondence between the *Directeur-Général* in Paris and the *Directeur* in Rome was long and detailed), and to the tapestry works at Gobelins and the State porcelain factories at Sèvres.

Yet even if the Crown and the State still remained the nominal patrons of contemporary art, the position had changed considerably since the previous reign. During the eighteenth century, private patrons rather than the Crown supplied the inspiration for the artists of the Rococo, though the origins of this style largely lay in the decorations of the royal palaces. The great outside forces in French art, in fact, were not the King and the court but wealthy financiers, such as Riche de la Popelinière and La Live de Jully, and cultivated amateurs and dealers, such as Jean de Jullienne and Mariette. It was largely they who either supported or combated the Rococo, which spread its curves and scrolls, its serpentine forms, over the face of architecture, painting and furniture. The Regency had witnessed the evolution of a style that was partly composed of French and partly of foreign influences. The Rococo, as Mr Fiske Kimball maintains, was a French style; it was French, however, only in so far as it appeared in the works of art produced in France or under her inspiration: elsewhere, in the Tiepolos at Würzburg, and Venice, and in much of the art of southern Germany and Austria, the Rococo flourished with those local differences and derivations that were to be expected. In France itself, the Rococo had, as we have seen, two distinct trends in painting and in decorative art. Boucher and Fragonard gave the Rococo its full expression in painting: Oppenord, Meissonier and Lajoue carried the Rococo to its ultimate destination in design.

The variety of the forms of art during the triumph of the Rococo was admirably reflected in the portraiture of the age. On the one hand, artists tended towards realism, as with Chardin and many of the portraitists; on the other, they became the creators of a world of mythology and suggestion. Inspired by this flight from reality, many court painters turned to the mythological portrait, a style in which few were as adept as Nattier. The vogue for this type of painting had begun in the seventeenth century; its popularity had increased owing to the influence of the theatre and the deification of woman as the centre of society. Charming, gracious and capable of flattery, this form of art had found its most accomplished exponent in Marc Nattier, that *élève des Graces* and *peintre de la beauté*, as Gresset termed him. He was the favoured artist of much of the aristocracy and the painter of those delightful but so flattering portraits of Mesdames de France, the King's daughters.

25

His portrait of the *Duchesse de Chartres en Hébé* was one of the great successes of the Salon of 1745, and may be compared with J. B. van Loo's no less characteristic portrait of the *Marquise de Sabran en Vénus*. The portraiture of both painters is spirited and full of atmosphere, if at times overblown; but in their drawings, particularly those of van Loo, their essential lack of vision is only too apparent.

Eighteenth-century portraiture was rich in all its aspects. Besides the conventional beauties of Boucher, Nattier and of the ever-attractive Madame Vigée-Lebrun, a more realistic manner of portrait-painting flourished. Chardin, Tocqué and Aved in the first half of the century, and later Donatien Nonotte and J. S. Duplessis, showed themselves capable of painting clearly observed portraits of the *bourgeoisie* and the upper classes. It was, too, one of the great periods of the pastel; beginning with Rosalba Carriera and Vivien, this subtle medium had attained particular delicacy and strength with Perronneau and Latour. Perronneau discovered his ideal subjects in charming and elegant women; as in his *Duchesse d'Ayen* (Louvre) the piquant expression of the face is completed by the soft shades of the dresses, those delicate mixtures of blue and yellow. Completely different in style is the radiant and brilliantly impulsive handling of Latour. A great psychologist, he observed and noted the personalities of his contemporaries with the insight of Laclos. His preparatory sketches, his *preparations*, are justly famous. He was singularly felicitous in his portraits of women, the lovely Mlle Fel, Madame de Pompadour and the delicious *Mlle Puvigné* (Pl. XXXVIII); but could also describe with only an indication the depths of a personality, the experience and humour of a man of the world such as *Crébillon* (Pl. XXXVII). His models believed, he once remarked, that he concentrated only on '*les traits de leurs visages, mais je descends au fond d'eux-mêmes à leur insu, et je les remporte tout entiers*'.[4] That was his special gift: with the swiftness of an epigram, he could assess the character of his sitters and leave an impression that was never to be forgotten: those unmistakable touches which, by indicating a Latour portrait, tempt us to know more and yet tell us all we need to know.

Latour represented the sardonic realism of the eighteenth century. Few artists in their works and personality so completely and characteristically expressed its predominant voluptuous qualities as François Boucher. He was the typical painter of his era. Prolific, pleasure-loving and gay, he lived and worked hard. Towards the end of his life Grimm described him as having the '*air d'un spectre et toutes les infirmités inévitables d'une vie consumée dans le travail et dans le déréglement des plaisirs*.'[5] The picture is perhaps unkind, but his words suffice to suggest the character of the man. He may perhaps have attempted too much and embraced too many aspects of the arts, instead of concentrating his energy on one activity, yet his very universalism reflected the spirit of his age. He desired to impress his personality on all the arts. He pandered perhaps to the tastes of a generation that loved pleasure, but then he was so pleasure-loving himself. If in his later productions he appears tired and over-ripe, in his best years few painters of his generation could rival the decorative quality of his composition and his sense of colour. In his old age, he was forced to witness a change in taste and the consequent fall from favour of his own work.

Yet, though his name has become associated with many legends and his work has suffered from many false attributions, he was a considerable figure. He was much more than a painter of artificial paradises and of faded decorations, weary of their own sensuality. He was industrious and competent. He may have deserved Bachaumont's stricture in the *Mémoires Secrets*, that he had '*un pinceau facile, agréable, spirituel et peut-être trop fin pour les détails champêtres auxquels il s'était consacré*',[6] yet he was an artist. He endowed the mythological style of painting with fire and energy. In his *The Rising* and *The Setting of the Sun* (London, Wallace Collection) he emerges as one of the great decorative artists of the age, able to submerge the billowing forms of his figures and the voluptuous tones of his painting to a unified whole; rhythmic, vital and dramatic, they anticipate Delacroix, the Delacroix of the decorations for the Chambre des Députés. Apart from his decorations, Boucher was pre-eminent as a brilliant draughtsman. His feeling for the nude was manifested in a supple and gracious exploration of form: he could render the least movements of the human figure (Pl. XLIV). The charm of his draughtsmanship is perpetual, and was immediately appreciated in his own day. To facilitate the sale of his drawings, he had them mounted on cartons; he was the first painter to exhibit drawings at the Salon, which he did in 1745. His variety was immense. He could turn from such fresh and spirited impressions of nature as that shown (Pl. V) to incisive illustrations for Molière, which caught the public taste by depicting Molière's characters in contemporary costume, or to drawings for the erotic tales of his friend, the Swedish Ambassador, Comte de Tessin, one of the best-known amateurs of the period, whose collection is now at the National Museum at Stockholm. Many-sided in his attitude to life—his drawings alone number over ten thousand—his very prolixity was a sign of his age: he gave himself unsparingly yet preserved, amidst the exigencies of his daily life, with its pleasures and labours, a standard that does not fail to impress. His humour and good nature, that appear in Cochin's portrait drawing of him, his sense of craftsmanship and his love of art, serve to deny Marmontel's unkind remark, that he was fitted to undertake only the lower sort of work.

Of his many activities, Boucher distinguished himself particularly as a designer of tapestries, those splendid pieces of Gobelins and Beauvais which are the real depository of decorative art during the eighteenth century. Those tendencies in decorative painting which had been announced by La Fosse, by Natoire in his decorations for the Hôtel de Soubise and by Lemoyne in the Salon d'Hercule at Versailles, made their most substantial appearance, not so much in Boucher's painting, as in the tapestry designed by him and his contemporaries. Some of his finest drawings were destined for tapestries, such as the seated violinist at Frankfurt on the Main, which is a study for *La Noble Pastorale*. His work in this field alone would be sufficient to distinguish him for posterity. How, indeed, he found time to act as Oudry's successor as Director of the Gobelins works between 1755 and 1770 and to design no less than forty models for the Beauvais works between 1736 and 1755 is truly amazing. Yet in these designs, he succeeded in adapting his style to the special requirements of the tapestry; and his *Fêtes Vénétiennes*, the *Histoire de Pysche*, the *Teinture Chinoise*, the *Nouvelle Teinture des Indes, Les Amours des Dieux, Les Frag-*

27

ments d'Opéra and *La Noble Pastorale* show a constant delicacy and solicitude for decoration. They compress into the myriad shreds of tapestry the golden strands of love and happiness that run through the age; they celebrate the pleasure and gaiety of the time when, as the Goncourts declared, '*partout se répand un raffinement d'élégance, une délicatesse de volupté*'.[7]

As *Premier Peintre*, however, Boucher had neither the force nor, one would suspect, the inclination to impose a definite programme on French art. He was no leader: he was too *aimable*. He preferred to be the favourite painter of Madame de Pompadour, to whom he imparted the rudiments of drawing. He preferred to leave to her the task of directing the course of French painting. To write of the art of this period, indeed, without taking her into account, would be a regrettable oversight. She personified so much of her age: her personal charm was reflected in its art. Despite the demands on her time entailed by her position, her ill-health, and her political intrigues, she was always prepared to patronize the arts. Her energy was amazing: she had the vitality which runs through the period and is consummated in Houdon's bust of Voltaire. Interested from her youth in art, letters and the stage, she enjoyed, as Royal Mistress, the power and wealth which were necessary to carry out her wishes. She defended Crébillon and gave her support to the *Encyclopédie* at a critical moment. Her energy imparted life to the Sèvres work; and their compliment in christening one of their most exquisite wares *Rose Pompadour* after her was well deserved. She had that rare gift of being able to impress a conception of art upon her age, of being able to call out the best in her contemporaries. It may well be that Marie Lecinska, tucked away in her apartments at Versailles, had as shrewd a notion of art as the King's *amie nécessaire*, as Duclos well called her, and that her taste for fine works was as cultivated and as sincere; but it was of little consequence. Madame de Pompadour had personality: she could infuse her own enthusiasm into her surroundings. An impresario of talent, she was always eager to stimulate, always ready to devote herself to art. She was aided in her pursuit by the psychological needs of her position: her desire to rivet the King's attention on her own personality, to amuse and interest him, meant that she was always on the move, always building and redecorating. In the same way, many of the jewels, caskets, *brûle-parfums* and pieces of furniture which she obtained from the jeweller, Lazare Duvaux, were designed to gain support from friend and foe alike—as when she sent her portrait, set in jewels, to Count Kaunitz, the Austrian Foreign Minister. Lazare Duvaux's account books, as Courajod well emphasized, are sidelights on the secret diplomacy of the period.[8]

By her position and her taste, Madame de Pompadour occupies a central position in eighteenth-century culture, and symbolizes its gaiety and elegance. Yet if she helped to direct patronage and taste through her personal influence wielded by the appointment of her relatives to the post of *Directeur des Beaux-Arts*, and if she summed up the Rococo at its maturity, she was not, and could not hope to be, the only source of artistic support in the country. Versailles was still important but the artistic development of the country took place, above all, in Paris. Paris had already assumed her position as the European centre of art, so that by the early years of the nineteenth century, Tom Moore could justly maintain that if Rome was the muse of art, Paris was the nurse. It was there that the amateurs and connoisseurs lived and, by the middle of the century, painters and engravers could exist on the commands given them by the nobility, the middle class and the dealers.

Art-dealing had now assumed considerable proportions in Paris. The knowledge and taste of the principal dealers in paintings, drawings and prints was considerable, and their influence generally beneficial. They published scholarly and well-documented catalogues, tastefully printed and embellished with elegant engravings, which were usually available in London. Such dealers as Mariette, Basan, Hell, Gersaint and Jullien exercised a decided influence on taste; Mariette, for instance, proclaimed a love for classical Italian art at a time when its popularity had waned in France. Nearly all lovers of drawings, they were quick to appreciate the beauty of an artist such as Watteau. It was typical of their harmonious relations with artists that Boucher designed Gersaint's business card, and Watteau his shop sign.

To collect was now a prerequisite of the noble or would-be noble, and Saint-Aubin and Demachy have left vivid drawings of sales in progress (Pl. XXXIII). Paris was now a cosmopolitan centre, and amongst the many foreign collectors who bought there themselves or through agents were Frederick II, the Russian Count Stroganoff, and Lord Spencer, who once owned Boucher's famous recumbent nude in the Ecole des Beaux Arts. The contents of these collections as they appear today from their sale catalogues throw much light on the development of contemporary taste. They show, for instance, that Dutch and Flemish painting continued to attract many collectors throughout the century. The collection of Randon de Boisset, who journeyed throughout Holland with Boucher as his artistic adviser, was particularly rich in examples of these schools. The collection of La Live de Jully, on the other hand, indicated the emergence of Neo-Classicism during the second half of the century; in his catalogue (1764), he described his rooms as being 'orné de meubles composés dans le style antique ou, pour me servir du mot dont on abuse si fort actuellement, dans le goût grec. . . .'[9] These catalogues are also particularly valuable in indicating the types of drawing collected by contemporary amateurs. The catalogue of the Randon de Boisset collection, for instance, shows that its owner possessed, not only drawings by Berghem, Ostade, Rubens, Van Dyck and Wouverman, but by Parmegianino and Raphael. The Quentin de Lorangère catalogue, too, lists drawings by artists as various as Bril, Lievens, Ruysdael, Goltzius, Rembrandt and Rubens, as well as numerous Italian works by Castiglione, Guido Reni, Salvator Rosa, Guercino and Bernini. Yet another collection rich in Dutch and Flemish art was that of W. Neyman, which was sold by auction in Paris in 1776.

Few groups in French society showed themselves to be such avid collectors and benevolent patrons as the rich financiers of the period, particularly the Fermiers-Généraux. Ever since Jacques Coeur, French financiers had interested themselves in the arts, and if, in the early years of the century, their rapacity and vulgarity was satirized, by the middle period, the Fermiers-Généraux had established a reputation as genuine and disinterested

29

amateurs of art. On occasion, it is true, their relations with their artists showed lack of understanding. The financier Bergeret, for instance, who had taken Fragonard with him on a tour of Italy in 1773, had expected that the artist would cede him all the drawings made while they were together. Fragonard did not agree. The decision of the lawsuit, which followed, showed an interesting appreciation of the particular relations that should exist between Maecenus and artist: Fragonard was authorized to keep his drawings, unless Bergeret was prepared to buy them from him for thirty thousand francs. Their quarrel was fortunately soon healed, and later, Fragonard spent some of his happiest and most productive hours at Bergeret's country place at Cassan, near Isle-Adam.

Bergeret's anxiety to secure Fragonard's drawings was not only a tribute to the artist himself but a sign of the growing prestige enjoyed by contemporary drawings. The drawing was now valued for its own sake, as an independent work of art. This interest is shown as much as anywhere else in the fascinating lecture on the *Dessin*, given by that loquacious amateur, the Comte de Caylus, to the Académie de Peinture in 1732.[10] It bears analysis in some detail. The drawing was for Caylus the basis for all artistic activity. He began by explaining that he intended to talk not only about this aspect of the drawing, which recalled the doctrines of the Poussinistes, but of *'les dessins en général, sur leur attrait, sur leur utilité et sur le connoissance'*.[11] As Caylus made the point that all the forms of art and all the productions of great men were interesting both for their contemporaries and for posterity, it seemed as if some sort of apology were still needed for an exclusive study of drawings. Drawings, he explained, had been sought for long; their importance to the painter and amateur of art was considerable; it is certain that one is *'fort avancée dans la connoissance des arts lorsqu'on les sait bien lire'*.[12] In a remarkable passage, which illuminates the contemporary conception of the drawing, he declared, *'Quoi de plus agréable, en effet, que de suivre un artiste du premier ordre dans le besoin qu'il a eu de produire, ou dans la première idée dont il a été frappé pour une machine dont on peut comparer l'exécution; d'approfondir les différents changements que ses réflexions lui ont fait faire avant d'avoir arrêté son ouvrage, de chercher à s'en rendre compte; de se voir enfin avec lui dans son propre cabinet, et de pouvoir se former le gout en examinant les raisons qui l'ont engagé à faire des changements. Après avoir admiré ces premières pensées, avec quel plaisir ne voit-on pas les études correctes faites d'après la nature, le nu d'une figure drapée, le détail de ce même draperie, enfin toutes les parties qui ont servi à la perfection du tableau ou de la machine que l'univers admire. Il me paroit encore que les grands artistes nous font éprouver des impressions semblables à celles qu'ils ont eux-mêmes ressenties: la poésie nous échauffe dans leurs premières conceptions, la sagesse et la vérité nous frappent dans les choses arrêtées.'*[13] The drawing contained, therefore, the possibility of being one of the most expressive artistic forms: it enabled the spectator to complete it in his own imagination. Yet, the pleasure derived from drawing meant that many painters neglected painting for its charms. With that desire to encourage historical painting, which inspired all Caylus's pronouncements, he maintained that painters *'se sont uniquement livrés au charme flatteur de jeter promptement leurs idées sur le papier, aussi bien qu'à celui d'imiter la nature*

30

dans les paysages et dans les autres beautés dont elle sait si bien piquer le goût de ses adora-teurs.' To draw, he continued not without wit, *'est toujours une espèce de libertinage que l'on doit blâmer, c'est un inconvénient dans lequel il faut surtout empêcher la jeunesse de tomber, avec d'autant plus de sévérité que cette habit d'augmenter chaque jour l'éloignement que l'on prend pour la peinture.'*[14] True as it was that the artist should form his style on the study of nature, beautiful as nature certainly was, it needed to be corrected by comparison with art; here, indeed, first-class drawings played their part.

Caylus's strictures may have seemed deserved. For many of the most talented artists of the century, the Moreaus and Cochins, were draughtsmen. That they were able to deploy their talent, their brilliant line and incisive statement, was largely due to the increased demand for book illustrations and engravings. A taste for finely printed books was and always has been a characteristic of the French, and a collector such as Madame de Verrue (one of the few women bibliophiles, as Andrew Lang once pointed out) possessed a library of over eighteen thousand volumes. To this cultivated and wealthy generation, books had to be handsomely produced, well bound, and embellished with choice engrav-ings. During the period, book illustration became a great repository of talent. The taste for book illustration had received support from the Regent, who himself illustrated *Daphnis et Chloë* (1718). It was further stimulated by Gillot with his engravings from the *Fables* of La Motte, which had something of the vivacity of the period, though as one wit observed:

> *'Quand le graveur Gillot et le poète Houdart*
> *Pour illustrer la fable auront mis tout leur art,*
> *C'est une vérité très sure*
> *Que le poète Houdart et le graveur Gillot*
> *En fait de vers et gravures*
> *Nous feront regretter La Fontaine et Callot.'*[15]

In the same period, too, Pater had illustrated Scarron's *Roman comique*. But it was not until the first quarter of the century was over that Boucher's six volume edition of Molière, containing figures in contemporary costume, gave a spur to the type of illustra-tion that was to typify the period. Boucher himself was an exception to the general rule. It was not generally the painters who devoted themselves to illustrating books but special engravers and draughtsmen, such as Eisen, Gravelot, Cochin and Moreau. Their work is sometimes unequal in quality. Eisen, for instance, excelled in small miniature illustra-tions, especially in those of a slightly licentious character, as in his drawings for Dorat's *Les Baisers*; and his drawing is precise and elegant. Gravelot, on the other hand, was often lifeless and insipid, though even he could produce such vivid sketches as his *Ballroom* at Oxford, and the *Rotunda*, once in the Heseltine collection, drawn in England where his influence was considerable. Cochin, too, could brilliantly suggest the atmo-sphere of a scene, as in his theatrical sketches or in his *Return from the Ball* (Oxford, Ashmolean). Of all the illustrators, none perhaps was as accomplished as Moreau le jeune, who, in his two styles, expressed the division between the two halves of the century. Called by his contemporaries *Le Boeuf*, he could turn from sketches of the King supping at Louveciennes (Pl. XXXI) or of domestic scenes in Parisian society (as in his drawings for the *Monument du Costume*, many of which are in the United States) to illustrations for Rousseau, and of the festivities of the Revolution. These artists were, however, only the cream of a gifted generation, which included accomplished minor figures, such as Choffard who excelled in designs for the *cul de lampe*.

Often brilliant, always talented, these *petits maîtres* failed to achieve the highest ranges of draughtsmanship. Too often they remained wedded to a delineation of the details of a story: they did not possess that richness and profusion of effect which Fragonard succeeded in achieving in his drawings for Tasso and Ariosto. However charming the drawings of Cochin, for instance, appear, he was prepared to sacrifice his personality and adopt the Neo-Classical form which barely reflected his own particular style.

Yet there is one exception to this general criticism, Gabriel de Saint-Aubin. He was a master of exquisite taste. He painted only a few pictures and was essentially a draughtsman, at his best in tender, delicate sketches, as in his study of a nude on a couch, redolent with atmosphere. An artist of evocation, he could distil into his softly tinted drawings the intimacy of a moment of happiness, as in his celebrated drawing *Réunion sous les Orangers* in the Ecole des Beaux-Arts, Paris (Pl. LXII). His figures palpitate with life, with warmth, with sensibility. To compare this drawing with Oudry's sketch of a similar scene in the same collection is to remark the degree of difference in their realism. Oudry presents a period piece in eighteenth-century costume, meticulous and correct; for Saint-Aubin, the scene transcends the commonplace, to become the symbol of a moment of ripe perfection.

Saint-Aubin's own self-portrait in his fascinating sketch book (Louvre) reveals a sensitive, humorous face, faintly mocking and always alert (Pl. XLV). Keenly receptive to the many facets of life, he was that typical Parisian figure, the *flâneur* whose life is bound by a love of his native city. In his celebrated sketchbooks, which are the linear diaries of the epoch, he noted down the pictures that passed in the sale rooms and could never resist scribbling sketches of them on the edges of his sale catalogues. He drew the architecture of Paris, attended its Balls, and revealed its hundred delights. He is the poet of Paris, and his absorption in the life of the boulevards, which was shared by artists such as Desrais, Meunier and Carle Vernet (Pls. XVI, VII, I), reflected that intense affection for the capital which again flowered in the following century in the art of Daumier and Meryon.

NOTES TO CHAPTER III

[1] *Le Style Louis XV*, Paris, 1942, p. 19.

[2] 'Each century has its own spirit which characterizes it. The spirit of our century is that of liberty.'

[3] The Académie de Saint-Luc, though managing to gain a confirmation of its rights in 1723, 1730 and 1738, never enjoyed the same prestige as the Académie Royale.

[4] ' . . . their features, but without their knowing it, I penetrate to their very depths, and carry them away in their entirety.' L. S. Mercier, *Tableau de Paris*, Amsterdam, 1782–1788, Vol. II. Cited by E. and J. de Goncourt, *L'Art du XVIII Siècle*, Paris, Vol. I, pp. 361–2.

[5] ' . . . air of a ghost and all the inevitable infirmities of a life spent in work and disordered pleasures.'

[6] 'A brush that was ready, pleasing, witty and perhaps too refined for the rural details to which he had devoted himself.'

[7] 'Everywhere there is diffused a refined elegance and a delicate sense of pleasure.' E. and J. de Goncourt, *op. cit.*, Vol. I, p. 196.

[8] *Livre-Journal de Lazare Duvaux* (1745–58). Edited by L. Courajod. Paris, 2 vols., 1873.

[9] 'Furnished in the antique style or, to employ a word that is so abused nowadays, in the Greek style.'

[10] Printed in *Conférences de Peinture et de Sculpture*. Ed. Henry Jouin. Paris, 1883, pp. 369–377.

[11] 'Drawings in general, of their charm, of their use, and of connoisseurship.'

[12] ' . . . much advanced in the knowledge of the arts when one knows how to understand them.'

[13] 'What indeed is more agreeable than to follow an artist of the first order in the urge which has driven him to create, or to compare his first conception with its final execution; to penetrate the various changes which his reflections have led him to make before the completion of his work, and to try to understand them; in short to be with him in his own study, and to be able to form one's own taste by examining the reasons which have caused him to make changes. After having admired his first thoughts, what a pleasure it is to observe the corrected studies taken from nature, the nude form of a draped figure, the detail of the very drapery, in a word, all the parts which have contributed to the perfect picture or machine which the whole world admires. Further, it seems to me that the great artists make us experience impressions similar to those which they themselves have felt. Poetry excites us in their first conceptions, wisdom and truth strike us in the finished works.'

[14] ' . . . have given themselves up entirely to the flattering charm of casting their ideas swiftly on paper, as well as to that of imitating nature in landscapes and in the other beauties, with which she can so well excite the taste of her adorers.' . . . 'is always a kind of profligacy that we ought to censure; it is an impropriety from which youth must at all costs be guarded with all the greater severity since this habit increases every day the neglect into which painting has fallen.'

[15] 'After the engraver Gillot and the poet Houdard have employed all their art to illustrate the fable, it is undeniable, in the matter of verses and engravings, that the poet Houdart and the engraver Gillot will make us regret La Fontaine and Callot.' E. Dacier, 'Claude Gillot', in *Les Peintres français du XVIIIe Siècle*. Edited by Louis Dimier. Paris-Bruxelles, 1928, 2 vols. Vol. I, p. 194.

IV. FORWARD TO REVOLUTION

GABRIEL DE SAINT-AUBIN's draughtsmanship was distinguished by its power to evoke and suggest atmosphere—above all the atmosphere of interiors and of groups of figures seen against the background of Paris. Yet, though essentially an artist of the city, some of his drawings reflect a preoccupation with nature, the effects of light and of the seasons. This interest in nature found increasing expression in the eighteenth century, in art, in literature and in life itself; here France anticipated the following generation, just as, across the Channel, the poetry of Cowper and the painting of Richard Wilson lead on to that of the Romantics.

French painters had in the past frequently shown a love for nature; and Poussin and Claude left romantic, nostalgic renderings of the Italian landscape. Later, in the first part of the eighteenth century, when the general tendency was on the whole for a return to the delights of the city, after exile at Versailles, this love of nature reappeared. In his land-scape backgrounds and in his drawings (Pl. X), Watteau showed a deep understanding for the quality of trees, their softness and shimmer. His contemporaries, too, Desportes and Oudry, drew or painted nature without any adornment. Oudry, in particular, showed the same fresh spirit in his drawings (Pl. VIII) which is so noticeable in the fascinating natural-ism of his painting of the *White Duck*, belonging to Lady Cholmondely, and the two still-lifes in the Wallace Collection.

Until the middle of the eighteenth century, however, a direct approach to nature on the part of artists was the exception, rather than the rule. In his *Discours sur le pratique de la peinture*, published in 1752, Oudry considered it necessary to admonish his pupils thus: '*Je voudrois, oui, je voudrois, quand vous auriez à faire un tableau dont la scène seroit en pleine campagne, que vous vous y transportassiez avec deux or trois amis bien unis par l'amour du travail; qu'après avoir trouvé un aspect ou un effet à peu près convenable à votre sujet, vous vous missiez à en faire quelques bonnes études, tant par rapport à la forme et la lumière que même pour la couleur; qu'ayant bien arrêté vos plans, vous missiez dessus quelques figures dans les endroits où vos auriez dessein de les placer dans votre com-position, pour voir l'effet qu'elles y feroient et par leur couleur et par leur grandeur. Deux d'entre vous, ou quelques-uns pris sur les lieux, peuvent remplir cet objet, parce que vingt figures ou une, c'est le même principe. J'espère que vous sentez que, moyennant ces précautions, vous ferez des choses au-dessus de ce que l'on fait communément, et que vous acquerrez un fond de principes et d'intelligence qu'on ne peut espérer de trouver dans le simple raisonnement.*'[1]

During the second half of the eighteenth century, this taste for nature, so carefully suggested by Oudry, became a normal element of the artist's baggage. In writing, the tendency was similar. A feeling for nature had, it is true, already been shown by Madame de Sévigné and La Fontaine, but only accidentally. Yet the excessive rationalization and urbanism of the *Philosophes* provoked inevitable opposition; and Rousseau, whose influence on painting was considerable, led in the reaction. With Rousseau, nature, and man's subjective reaction to it, held the stage. It was the exaltation of the sentiment that man, born good, happy, and corrupted only by the evils of society, could regain his lost innocence in communion with nature—not with nature at its most sublime but in the woods, hills and lakes. The same sort of nostalgic love for nature marks Moreau l'aîné. He turned to the neighbourhood of Paris, finding his themes in the silvery qualities and the gentle atmosphere of Bagatelle and of the Château de Madrid where the repose of some rustic retreat provided a compensation for the bustle of Paris (Pl. XIII).

A desire to render the delights of nature was shared by two of the most important painters of the second half of the eighteenth century, by Fragonard and Hubert Robert. Both drew their inspiration from Italy as much as from France, from the swaying cypresses and the perfumed air of the Villa d'Este (Pl. XI). Once again that fruitful relationship that had existed between the two countries bore fruit, once again French artists, who had learnt much from Italy, where they studied in the Académie at Rome, were only too happy to repay their debt with works which evoked the very nature of Italy and yet remained essentially French. No longer did they feel in an inferior position in regard to their great neighbour: the Rococo had arrived—a style that was impregnated with the French spirit, a style that was their own.

Both artists were to react against the Rococo style; yet both were also to stem from it. They radiated the spirit of the Rococo in their lightness and elegance, but at the same time they felt no need to engage in the curves and pirouettes of Meissonier or Oppenord. They were straightforward and direct. They were similar, too, in that they both found the road to Italy at an early date. Fragonard had gone to Rome at the age of twenty-seven. There he had studied at the Académie and was considered to be a promising pupil by the Director, Charles Natoire, whose sketch of the students at work vividly recalls the atmosphere of the school (Pl. LVIII). He met, above all, the Abbé de Saint Non (Pl. XX), one of the most engaging amateur artists of the period, and he made the acquaintance of Hubert Robert. Robert was already painting those pictures of ruins which were to make him so celebrated. All three made friends. They were an ideal group, painting and drawing together. They settled in the Villa d'Este, which the Abbé de Saint Non had been lent by his friend, the Duke of Modena. There they drew their innumerable sketches of its gardens, those exquisite red chalk evocations of the luscious qualities of Italy. For Fragonard, these were rich and crowded days. He made new contacts, meeting the Abbé Barthelemy, who attempted to provoke his interest in Neo-Classical art. He accompanied Saint Non to Naples, where he drew after the classical remains at Pompeii (as well as copying pictures); but he had found his right approach to painting in the direct inspiration from nature.

Fragonard could not remain for ever in Italy. He returned to Paris, where he was commissioned to execute an important historical painting for the Crown. Payment for this commission was exceedingly slow, and though Cochin, who admired his work, attempted to hasten the Directeur, he met with no success, and Fragonard was forced to turn elsewhere for his living. What direction his painting might have taken if he had been persuaded to become a history painter, if circumstances had forced him to adopt the Neo-Classical convention, must remain a matter for speculation. But he was now thrown on his own resources and free to develop his own style, to display his passionate exuberance in a manner of his own choice. By chance, he was asked to paint the celebrated *La Balançoire* (London, Wallace Collection) for the Baron Jullien, and quickly became the much sought-after master of *galant* and slightly licentious works. He adopted this sort of painting with enthusiasm, joining the rather raffish set of artists, writers, financiers and actresses who thronged the receptions given by La Guimard. He is said to have become her lover, and certainly agreed to paint a set of decorations for her house. Yet they parted, and Fragonard, when he realized that La Guimard expected him to paint for nothing, refused to continue the work which was eventually finished by David.

Fragonard is an artist of two faces. Of all his contemporaries, he gave the most sustained and aesthetic expression to Parisian gallantry—those exquisite drawings, *Ma chemise brûle*, *Le Verrou* (Pl. LIII) with their felicitous wash, their delicate pencil work. He was also the poet of rustic life, who distilled into his drawings the freshness, the freedom, of country pleasures, of love-making in the hay, of children playing in the stables. He could be at once elegant and substantial, as in his drawings of animals. He was essentially an artist of appreciation: there are no critical undertones, no questions in his work. His own enjoyment of life is contained in his drawings: they represent the rapid, unhampered moments of pleasure. His love was always for Italy, for the Baroque phase of its art, the richly painted impulsive style of Pietro da Cortona and Solimena. Drawing was for him, as it had been for Watteau and Saint-Aubin, a means of expression that came readily to hand. He drew naturally and spontaneously. '*Rond, replet, fringant, alerte, les joues rouges, les cheveux gris en désordre, les yeux pétillants, toujours vêtu au logis d'une houppelande ou roquelaure de drap gris sans agrafe, ni pattes, ni boutons, qu'il serre à la taille, au moment de peindre, à l'aide de n'importe quoi, bout de chiffon ou bout de ficelle,*'[2] wrote a contemporary of him when, in his later years, he lived in the Louvre. It is a description which gives much of the man and of his art. He moved over the pages of his drawings without embarrassment, taking in his stride the intimate details of the boudoir, or the frank announcements of love. He was a romantic, who relied on the spontaneous approach to life and to art; and his dramatic love affair with Rosalie Gerard, his sister-in-law, anticipates the passion of Prud'hon and Constance Mayer.

Fragonard dwelt on the positive qualities of Italy, the scented charm of those villas in which he drew and painted with such delight. Hubert Robert found his inspiration in its ruins, the romantic and picturesque elements of the past which he evoked so well (Pl. III). His formula was not new. It had been used before, by some Italian humanists of the fifteenth century and, in more recent times, by Piranesi and Pannini. Hubert Robert was, all the same, personal and sincere: his paintings have a lingering charm. Yet they have not the vivacity, the liveliness of Fragonard: his red chalk drawings (many of which were bequeathed by Paris the architect to the Besançon Museum) are frequently too carefully

36

composed and lack an essential spontaneity. He was, and will remain, a connoisseur of ruins, resurrecting, in the temples of the past, his own nostalgia and regret. He was, however, no dreamer; like so many of his contemporaries, he worked hard: as Madame Vigée-Lebrun said of him, '*il peignait un tableau aussi vite qu'il écrivait une lettre.*'[3] He had the facility that comes from a passionate desire to extract as much as possible from life.

Now that nature had become a source of inspiration, artists such as Boissieu, Desfriches Hoeul, Pillement, Maréchal, Valenciennes and Vernet (Pls. II, VI), found their most convincing means of expression, landscape or seascape. The taste for nature had become popularized by Saint-Non's publication of his monumental *Voyage Pittoresque à Naples* . . . in which Chatelet and Desprez collaborated, and by the appearance of prints after the series of views of French ports undertaken by Vernet for the Marquis de Marigny. A tendency to turn to nature was also apparent in the taste for picturesque gardens. The *Jardin Anglais* was favoured by many; by 1767, Rousseau had sketched a plan for one in the *Nouvelle Héloïse*. This retreat to the countryside, this return to a romantic feeling for nature took place in those charming country-houses, such as Moulin-Joli where Watelet lived in such peace and of which he must have thought in his essay, '*Essai sur Les Jardins*': '*Que d'autres bâtissent des palais pour enfermer leurs chagrins et établir leur vanité, je me suis fait une solitude pour amuser mes loisirs et causer avec mes amis.*'[4] This desire for an interesting solitude became fashionable: at Ermonville, at Betz (owned by the Princesse de Monaco), and in the Prince de Ligne's house at Belœil, the garden became the repository of that nostalgic longing for peace and solitude that dominates so much of the art and thought of the second half of the century, even before the appearance of Chateaubriand and the concept of the noble savage.

What is so curious about the century is its dualism. Together with the interest in nature came a revival of history painting and the appearance of the Neo-Classical style. History painting, indeed, had never altogether been submerged even during the years of reaction against Lebrun. In the early years of the century, for instance, the Duc d'Antin (then *Directeur des Beaux-Arts*) had instituted reforms in the teaching of art which aimed to preserve the practice of history painting. He had also tried to encourage painting in the 'Grand Manner' by giving commands to Lemoyne for the Salon de la Paix and the Salon d'Hercule at Versailles. All the time signs of this continuing interest appeared; Jean Restout finished his uncle's painting of the *Nouveau Testament*, and designs for tapestry such as J. F. de Troy's *Tenture d'Esther* and Charles Coypel's *Histoire d'Armide* maintained the historical tradition at the Gobelins works.

Orry, who succeeded D'Antin as Directeur, was a man of little imagination and small taste, with a keen desire to economize expenditure on the arts; but he did make some efforts to maintain the prestige of history painting. But, as the historian of this movement has pointed out,[5] to do this effectively, more would have had to be spent on art, and this Orry was disinclined to advise. He did realize, however, the importance to artists of reopening the Salon; this he did in 1737, the year he took office.

Circumstances, however, no less than a change in the direction of taste, helped to favour the restoration of historical painting and with it the development of the Neo-Classical style. Madame de Pompadour did much to effect this. However, she did not actively encourage Neo-Classicism as much as is often claimed, and it is certainly exaggerated to maintain, on the evidence of her copies after antique gems drawn by Leguay, and her acquaintance with Bouchardon, that she was the principal promoter of the movement. On the contrary, as Edmond de Goncourt observed, she specifically dictated the subject of the *Conversation Espagnole* to Van Loo, in order to free French painting from the tyranny of the schools, and to turn it in the direction of a portrayal of contemporary life. In the Neo-Classical movement, her role was accidental. It was, indeed, exercised through the nomination of her uncle and brother to the all-important posts of Directeurs-Généraux des Bâtiments.

Immediately after her uncle, LeNormant de Tournehem, was appointed to this post, he began to set about the renewal of this style—for example by nominating Charles Coypel to the post of *Premier Peintre*, which had lapsed since the death of its last incumbent, Lemoyne, in 1737. This meant not only that a painter, sympathetic to history painting, had reached a position of importance in the French administration: it meant the assumption of artistic power by that *éminence grise* the Abbé LeBlanc. He and Coypel were on the best of terms, and in his *Lettre sur les Beaux-Arts* LeBlanc had already declared war on the Rococo. Important measures indicated a general design to bolster up history painting. For this purpose, an Ecole Royale des Elèves Protegés was created to serve as a sort of preparatory school for the pupils of the Academy of Painting, where the young artist received tuition in history, mythology and iconology. At the same time, the prizes awarded to various artists were tacitly understood to be for those painters adopting the historical style. A further symptom of the Crown's considerable effort in this direction was that in 1747 the King ordered for Choisy eleven history paintings from the best painters in France. They were exhibited in the Salon du Louvre and included Restout's *Alexander*, Van Loo's *Silenus et Bacchus*, Dumont le Romain's *Mutius Scaevola*, Jeaurat's *Diogenes* and Collin's *Pyrrhus*.

This renewal of history painting was not hard to explain. Many people wanted to see a revival of the sense of history at a time when French prestige had begun to decline. One of Vien's works, for instance, was an allegory critical of Britain's belligerency. They also wanted some sort of counterbalance to the Rococo. In this transitional period, the painters of the *Grande Génération*, Cazes, Galloche and Louis de Silvestre, mingled with those of the middle years such as J. F. de Troy and Carle Van Loo: together they paved the way for Vien's Neo-Classical interpretation of history painting. The first public celebration of the Neo-Classical triumph came with the celebrated journey of the Marquis de Marigny to Italy in company with Cochin, Soufflot and the Abbé LeBlanc, his *yeux* as Marigny called them. Their tour was extensive. They saw much besides Rome, visiting Bologna, Florence, Venice and Naples. They spent some time at Herculaneum, though they did not admire the recently discovered paintings, then on view in the Palace of the Portici. Cochin, indeed, was to find that the paintings possessed a *composition froide*, and he adds *tableaux médiocrement dessinés 'faire pesant et froid'*.[6] Their colour was *mauvaise*. Yet, Cochin found much to please him in the sculpture and in the domestic utensils. Though the travellers certainly rejected much that was classical in feeling, their journey was important: French painting was now open to the infiltration of a Neo-Classical style.

In Italy and in England, Neo-Classicism was the style of the moment. It had begun as the result of an interest, half professional and half amateurish, in the origins of antiquity, as a branch of history. Such publications as Montfaucon's in France and Lord Burlington's edition of Palladio's drawings of Roman baths had acted as a stimulus to this taste, which found further support in Piranesi's *Antichità Romane* and *Varie Vedute* and the cult of ruins as a whole. Of even greater importance was the systematic excavation of Herculaneum, which began in 1738, and the operations at Pompeii some ten years later.

These publications had treated of the remains of Roman antiquity, but at the same time other archæologists and artists turned their attention to those of Greece. By 1750, Soufflot was measuring the ruins at Paestum; during the 'sixties appeared such important publications as Leroy's *Ruines des plus beaux monuments de la Grèce*, the first volume of Stuart and Revett's *Antiquities of Athens*, Major's *Paestum* and Winckelmann's *Geschichte der Kunst*, all of which exalted the supremacy of Greek art. How far these publications influenced the course of French art is still a matter of debate, and the most recent historian of the Rococo and of the Neo-Classical revival has argued that 'the stricter classical phase, appearing in France at the very end of Louis XV's reign, was strongly influenced by England.' In support of his claim, Mr Kimball has advanced a wealth of evidence: the publications of Campbell, the influence of English thought and the classical motives of much English architecture of the eighteenth century, do much to prove his case, though the direct relationship between France and Italy, the source for so much Neo-Classical feeling, was clearly of comparable importance.

In the introduction of this knowledge of classical art into France, and in the demand for its standards, an important part was played by the Comte de Caylus. If the taste for Neo-Classicism was already coming from England, he did much to stimulate it by publishing the finds at Pompeii in collaboration with Bellicard in 1754, and by his patronage and encouragement of various modern artists. A fascinating, if at times provoking figure, he mixed a deep attachment to his mother with a taste for archæology and a determined desire for dissipation. The author of numerous studies on art, he was also the composer of scurrilous and licentious verses. Vicious, proud and intolerant, Caylus was a personality. With his woollen stockings, his thick shoes, his brown cloth coat with its leather buttons, he was the very opposite of the dandified dilettante of the period. Undoubtedly he took himself too seriously, and the patronizing tone of his lectures to the Academy must have been provoking in the extreme. Yet he was shrewd and intelligent in many of his judgments and he had fire and passion in his love for the fine arts. He certainly earned the enmity of Cochin and Marmontel. Yet he had a contribution to make, and the man who could write that '*je goûte, après avoir dessiné, et plus de volupté avec ma maîtresse ou mes amis, et plus de calme dans l'esprit*'[7] was certainly not negligible. He threw all his energies into the support of a revival of the classical ideal, even going so far as to suggest that painting should utilize the technical processes employed by the ancients. His views were certainly exaggerated, though even he acknowledged that the artist should never forget to study nature. The very excess of his doctrine diminished the force of his arguments, which were conveyed with more wit and greater subtlety by Cochin in his celebrated *Lettres aux Orfèvres* and in the articles he wrote for the *Mercure de France* in 1754 and 1755.

Cochin demanded not so much a revival of classical forms as a return to the *bon goût du siècle précédent*; he expressly warned painters of the danger of too slavishly copying ancient painting and of relying on archæology. It was just this attempt to paint in a Greek manner, rather than to create a new and valid style, which tempted a painter such as Vien. During his stay in Rome, his painting barely indicated his later manner; once back in Paris he became an enthusiastic Neo-Classicist under the influence of Caylus. Today, his painting and drawing, though not without a certain charm, appear poor in quality and dull in conception; to many of his contemporaries, however, his use of *encaustique* seemed a correct and satisfactory manner of painting, and numbers of his drawings were published as engravings by his wife. Their popularity went to substantiate Grimm's remarks in the *Correspondance Littéraire*: '*Cet excès est ridicule sans doute, mais qu'importe? Si l'abus ne peut s'éviter, il vaut mieux que l'on abuse d'une bonne chose que d'une mauvaise.*'[8]

Vien's style was, however, not so influential in painting as that of history painting proper: and the artists of his generation, such as Challe, Lagrenée, Deshays, Doyen, worked in the Grand Manner with a greater or lesser use of classical motifs. Their work had a more robust personality, was richer in its effect. Doyen's painting of the *Peste d'Ardents*, for instance, the drawing for which is here reproduced (Pl. LVII), was impregnated with Rubens's influence and at the same time looked forward to Gros. Vincent, for instance, could produce a charming if sentimental sketch (Pl. LVI), and Deshays suggest a mythological scene with elegance (Pl. XVII).

Simultaneously with the appearance of Neo-Classicism and history painting came the idea that painting should convey a moral message; it was a natural development of the idea of history painting. In 1764, for instance, Cochin pointed out that painters had for so long represented the heroic actions of kings that they could as well paint those actions which had contributed under benevolent rulers to the happiness of their people. It was a significant statement. Art was clearly expected to convey a thesis; it was allowed to have a critical rôle. It was the dawn of the Revolution, the realization that art and literature could assist in the storming of the bastions of absolutism and orthodoxy. Paradoxically, history painting, which was encouraged to assist in the renewal of national energy, contained the seeds of that criticism which was to destroy the Crown: revolutionary art was the child of Neo-Classicism.

During the century as a whole, realism had formed one of the major elements in artistic creation. Again and again, the painters of the period indicated, above all in their drawings, that they could draw all classes and types with a realistic attitude. Even a painter such as Watteau, so commonly thought of as the artist of an aristocratic ideal alone, revealed in his drawings that he was a supreme realist. Bouchardon, on the other hand, who was one of the principal figures in the Neo-Classical revival, could also show himself to be a faithful recorder of the street scenes of Paris, as in his drawings for *Les Cris de Paris* in the British Museum. A minor artist such as the charming Carmontelle, whom we tend to associate with the restricted circles of the Orléans family at Chantilly, was much more than a sycophant. In his amusing miniature plays, which were performed at Chantilly, he did not hesitate to caricature the intellectual pretensions of the aristocracy and to compose brilliant studies of peasant life; he was, too, the draughtsman of delightful sketches of the circle at Chantilly or of that of Madame de Genlis, as in his drawing of Grimm and Diderot (Pl. XXVI).

In the seventeenth century, this realism had been at its best in the painting of the brothers Le Nain. It was to find a worthy successor in Chardin. He painted the life he knew and esteemed: the maid working in the kitchen, the hare suspended amongst the pots, the boy blowing soap bubbles, the card players. Yet there is no ulterior motive in his painting. Chardin treated such themes not, as Diderot would have desired, because he felt that they contained a literary or symbolical significance, but because they embodied the eternal truths of painting, the mysteries of formal relations, the weight and depth of objects set in their relation to space and their colour values. As Rilke so well said, he divested the eighteenth-century blue of its sophistication, and like Vermeer or Braque, played endless variations on the science of picture making. His drawings are few in number, but those that exist show many of his qualities; they reveal that he could seize the essence of a scene and render it with a rapidity, a brilliance, which belongs only to a great master. To compare his drawing of two men and the sedan chair at Stockholm (Pl. XLIX) and Gillot's study for the *Deux Carosses* is to see the difference between two conceptions: for Gillot the details intrigue, he can subordinate the elements to the whole; but the essential movement has to be guessed, is not conveyed. For Chardin, it is no longer a genre scene, no longer an essay in the picturesque; it is a chance to determine the relations of form within the confines of the drawing.

Chardin was in the nature of a test case for the eighteenth century. Had he been despised, had he been overlooked, who could have been surprised? His art was so much at variance with that of Boucher, Lancret and Pater. Yet, he was appreciated. Madame de Verrue included his works in her collection; they were sought by Parisian collectors and by foreign amateurs, such as the Comte de Tessin and the Prince de Liechtenstein. Yet, what could have been more typical of the second half of the century, what more revealing than that at first Diderot was reserved in his appreciation of Chardin's value, though by the 'seventies (1774) he had come round to acknowledge that he had succeeded in portraying *la nature même*, coupling him with Vernet as a *grand magicien*?

What Diderot sought, what indeed the writers and painters of the last part of the eighteenth century sought, was not so much the sincerity of Chardin, as the sentimentality of Greuze. Greuze himself was one of the most paradoxical of artists: a brilliant technician, he was corrupted by contemporary taste, befogged by the aesthetic theories of the moment, and much disturbed by the infidelities of his wife. As the portraitist of the brilliant Sophie Arnould, he was able to catch all her charm, the implied sensuality of her look. He could paint portraits that possess the richness and direct brilliance of Géricault and the Romantics. Yet, on the other hand, he was more often than not tempted to paint dreary, saccharine portraits abounding in allusions to the fallen virtues of young women, those doves with their broken jugs which can only provoke dismay. They lack an essential frankness, are too suggestive, and reflect that sense of playing with forbidden fruit which runs through Diderot's *La Religieuse*, which hints at but never directly avows the truth, that tradition of endless seduction which stems from *Pamela*. As a draughtsman, Greuze was often brilliant; his sense of line, his judgment of character was sure and precise. He could suggest, as in his portrait of the Duc d'Orléans, the depth of a character (Pl. XIX), or improvise some scene of a moral nature which was aided by his effective use of wash. He aimed at respectability, at the depiction of the domestic scenes and tribulations of the middle classes who were coming to play an ever-increasing part in the life of the country, and whose interiors were faithfully recorded by Greuze himself, by Jeaurat and Lepicié.

Greuze was sentimental, in a way which suited the middle classes. He told tales which never seemed far remote from their own experiences: the prodigal son, death-bed forgiveness. He did not possess that more aristocratic cult of the heart which, stemming from Rousseau, had gained possession of the court and those sentiments which were so charmingly expressed by Parny and would, one feels, have admirably suited the characters appearing in the portraits of Madame Vigée-Lebrun, Danloux and J. B. Lemoyne (Pls. XLVI, XXXIX). For all their sentimentality, how charming they are, these playthings of fate before the outburst of the Revolution. They formed the inhabitants of the unreal world of Versailles, which under Louis XVI had lost so much of the country's respect. The King himself was narrow and limited in his taste for art, and indifferent as a man of affairs. Capricious, volatile and indiscreet, the Queen offended by her frivolity and was the known tool of the Austrian party. She had little understanding for painting, and less taste, though her moral scruples occasioned her to remove from the old King's private rooms Boucher's last and most licentious decorations.

During the last part of the century, the gulf between the court and the people widened —or rather the people had begun to see the abuses of the court and of the social system more clearly. The latter part of the reign of Louis XV and that of Louis XVI form, indeed, a sharp contrast to the happy years of the middle period. The finances of the country, always in an uneasy condition, were now in a deplorable state, and the efforts of Turgot and Necker to remedy affairs only contributed to the general discredit. At least in foreign affairs, however, one of the most brilliant diplomatists of the period, Vergennes, the Foreign Minister, managed to extract some advantage for France from the American War of Independence. Success abroad, though welcome, was hardly sufficient compensation for the internal condition of France; inevitably the country was to incur some form of crisis. In the past, dissatisfaction had been considerable, but it had now become vocal. During the eighteenth century, however, public opinion began to emerge as an important factor, stimulated by the philosophers and other writers. Its spearhead was the middle class. '*Deux grandes forces, à la fin du XVIIIe siècle,*' wrote Jean Jaurès in his *Histoire Socialiste de la Révolution Française*, '*deux forces révolutionnaires ont passioné les esprits et les choses et multiplié par un coefficient formidable l'intensité des événements. Voici ces deux forces: D'une part, la nation française est arrivée à la maturité intellectuelle. D'autre part, la bourgeoisie française est arrivée à la maturité sociale. La pensée française avait pris conscience de sa grandeur et elle voulait appliquer à la réalité toute entière, à la société comme à la nature, ses méthodes d'analyse et de déduction. La bourgeoisie française avait pris conscience de sa force, de sa richesse, de son droit, de ses chances presque indéfinies de développement.*'[9] In effect, it was this *bourgeoisie* who, by striving to limit the powers of the privileged classes and to assert their own will-power, contributed to the final conflagration and to the fall of the Bourbons.

This new movement towards liberty of expression and expansion did not fail to affect the arts. Above all, David stood out as the great champion of the revolutionary and Republican ideals, alike in his declarations and in his painting. He had begun life as a conventional painter of the eighteenth century, a recorder of its *galanteries*, and had succeeded Fragonard as the decorator of Mlle Guimard's apartments. But as a pupil of Vien, he was in the direct line of descent from Neo-Classicism, although when staying in Rome it was only after considerable hesitation that he endorsed the ideas of Mengs, Winckelmann and Canova. In 1779, for instance, he made the conventional journey to Naples with the painter Suzanne and the critic Quatremère de Quincy, and on his return to France in the following year he was completely converted to the ideals of the new school, painting his celebrated *Les Horaces* despite the opposition of d'Angiviller, the Directeur des Beaux-Arts.

In many of his early works, David had shown himself only too pleased to accept the orders given him by members of the aristocracy, but, also, as in his fine portrait of Count Potocki (Willanow, A. Branicki), he could command a brilliantly naturalistic approach. With the outbreak of the Revolution, amidst all the exciting days of 1789, he emerged as a strong supporter of the Revolutionary party, anxious not only to transform the political complexion of the country, but to break down what appeared to him to be the tyranny of the Academy. In his sketches for the *Serment au Jeu de Paume*, he celebrated the Revolution at its most splendid, and at its constitutional, moments. In his first sketches for this composition, he managed to convey the impact of the groups with palpitating visual excitement: the frieze of figures is endowed with the spontaneity of a direct experience, transposed though they are into another era. In the second stage of preparatory sketches, the scene is frozen into place, made glacial and firm, unbending and inevitable like the Revolution itself.

David himself played a considerable role in the Revolution, and one not always to his credit. It is true that he saved his old friend Fragonard from the guillotine, but he made no move to help Sedaine. He was implacable. As a member of the Convention, of the

Committee of Public Instruction, and of the Committee of Public Safety, he was one of the moving forces in events, though in the end he, too, fell into disgrace. Cold and opportunist as a man, he was brilliant as a painter. He could distil the essence of a scene —as in his sketch of Marie-Antoinette on the way to the guillotine. With her curled lips, her bedraggled expression, even David is unable to deny that she is a regal figure, though his own prejudices are apparent in the malice of the sketch.

In David, Neo-Classicism found its sublimation, its proper expression. David, and David alone, could infuse vitality into a style which was so often academic and dull. He saw that in the legends and example of the Republics of Greece and Rome lay a message for his own generation: the exaltation of public spirit at the expense of personal desire. The *Brutus* of David's painting, said the Marxist critic George Plekhanov, is a paterfamilias, 'but a paterfamilias who has become a citizen. His morality is the political morality of a revolutionary.' He shows how far *bourgeois* France has travelled since the time when Diderot extolled Greuze because of the moral tendency of his work.[10] The next step in the evolution of France, the dictatorship of Napoleon, found David perfectly prepared to follow his doctrine. There was no need for a break in David's art: as his drawing of *Napoleon and the Sacre* shows (Pl. XLVIII), he now exalted the supremacy not of the People and the State but of the State vested in the person of one man.

From the artistic point of view, what was so important about David was his ability to render scenes with dramatic realism. Not only was he the chronicler of the heroic days of the Revolution and the First Empire, but he was the painter of the astonishing portrait of an old woman in the Louvre which anticipates Courbet and is practically a new departure in French painting. In his art, the eighteenth century had come full circle. The authority of the Committee of Instruction, of Napoleon, was substituted for that of the Academy and Louis XIV, which had obtained at the beginning of the century. The happy and gay art of the Régence and of the Rococo surrendered to the didactic and moral painting of the Revolutionary era. Much of the old régime was still to linger on, in France or abroad, where the emigré painters, Madame Vigée-Lebrun and Danloux (Pl. XXXIX), preserved the graces of the past; and they were to regain some of their former position under the Restoration. The century, indeed, was to end on a positive note. In his fascinating drawings of Josephine (Pl. LX), Prud'hon expressed all the tenderness and the introspection of the Romantics, and David, too, in such drawings as the portraits of M. and Madame Lenoir (Pl. XL) indicates the vigorous realism of the Revolution. Despite the Revolution, despite the turmoil of war, continuity was to be preserved. Great in its own right, pregnant with the seeds of much that was to come, the eighteenth century drew to a close, that century which the Goncourts termed so rightly the century '*le plus essentiellement français de notre histoire nationale*'.[11]

[1] 'I strongly advise that whenever you have to paint a picture with a scene set in the open country, you go there with two or three friends united by a common love of work; and that once you have found an aspect or an effect more or less suited to your subject, you set a few figures in the positions you intend them to occupy in your composition, to give you an idea of their effect there from the point of view of colour and size. Two of you, or any one found on the spot, can serve this purpose, because the principle is the same whether you have one figure or twenty. By means of these precautions, I hope that you feel that you may achieve something above the average, and that you will acquire a basis of principles and understanding which one cannot hope to find in the simple process of reasoning.'

[2] 'Round, corpulent, lively, alert, his cheeks flushed, his grey hair disordered, his eyes sparkling, in his rooms always dressed in an overcoat or cloak of grey cloth, without hooks, tabs or buttons, which he ties round himself while he paints with anything that comes to hand, a piece of rag or string.' Cited by Pierre de Nolhac, *Fragonard 1738–1806*, Paris, 1918, p. 165.

[3] 'He painted a picture as quickly as he wrote a letter.'

[4] 'Let others build palaces to confine their sorrows and establish their vanity. I have made a solitude for myself in which to amuse my hours of leisure and talk with my friends.'

[5] J. Locquin, *La Peinture d'Histoire en France de 1747 à 1785*, Paris, 1912.

[6] '. . . mediocrely designed, appearing heavy and cold.' Charles-Nicholas Cochin, *Voyage d'Italie ou Recueil des Notes sur les Ouvrages de Peinture et de Sculpture qu'on voit dans les principales Villes d'Italie*, Paris, 1758, cited by Fiske Kimball, *op. cit.*, p. 200.

[7] 'After I have drawn, I enjoy more pleasure with my mistress or with my friends, as well as more calm in my mind.' E. Raunié, *Souvenirs et Correspondance de Mme de Caylus*, Paris, 1881, p. 309.

[8] 'No doubt this excess is absurd, but what does it matter? If abuse is inevitable, better abuse of a good thing than of a bad one.'

[9] 'At the end of the eighteenth century, two great revolutionary forces inflamed men's minds and formidably increased the intensity of events. On the one hand, the French nation had reached intellectual maturity. On the other hand the French *bourgeoisie* had reached social maturity. French thought had become conscious of its greatness, and wished to apply to the whole of reality, to society as well as to nature, its method of analysis and deduction. The French *bourgeoisie* had become conscious of its strength, its wealth, its rights, its almost indefinite chances of development.'

[10] 'French Drama and Painting of the Eighteenth Century' in *Art and Society* (trans. Alfred Goldstein. Introduction Granville Hicks), New York, 1936, p. 27.

[11] 'The most essentially French century of our national history.'

BIBLIOGRAPHY

CAYLUS, Comte de. *Vie d'Artistes du XVIIIe Siècle*. (Ed. A. Fontaine. Paris, 1910.)

CHENNEVIÈRES, H. de. *Les Dessins du Louvre*. (Paris, 1882-1884.)

COGNIAT, R. *Le Dessin français au XVIIIe Siècle*. (Monaco, 1943.)

DACIER, E. *Le Style Louis XVI*. (Paris, 1939.)

DILKE, Lady C. *French Painters of the XVIIIth Century*. (London, 1899.)

DILKE, Lady C. *French Engravers and Draughtsmen of the XVIIIth Century*. (London, 1902.)

DUMESNIL, M. J. *Histoire des plus célèbres Amateurs français et de leur Relations avec les Artistes*. (Paris, 3 vols., 1856-1858.)

GILLET, Louis. *Histoire des Arts en France* (in *Histoire de la Nation Française*, ed. G. Hanotaux. (Paris, 1922.)

GONCOURT, E. & J. de. *L'Art français du XVIIIe Siècle*. (Paris, 3 vols., 1881-1882.)

GUIFFREY, J., & MARCEL, P. *Inventaire-général des Dessins des Musées du Louvre et du Musée de Versailles (Ecole française)*. (Paris, 10 vols., 1908-1921.)

HOURTICQ, L., DACIER, E., BOUYER, R., JAMOT, P., and BRIÈRE, G. *Le Paysage français de Poussin à Watteau*. (Paris, 1928.)

LAVALLÉE, P. *Les Dessins français du XVIIIe Siècle à l'Ecole des Beaux-Arts*. (Brussels, 1928.)

PELOUX, Vicomte Charles de. *Répertoire biographique et bibliographique des Artistes du XVIIIe Siècle français*. (Paris, 2 vols., 1930-1941.)

PORTALIS, Baron R. de. *Les Dessinateurs d'Illustrations au XVIIIe Siècle*. (Paris, 2 vols., 1877.)

VAILLAT, L. *La Société du XVIIIe Siècle et ses Peintres*. (Paris, 1912.)

WILDENSTEIN, G. *Le dix-huitième Siècle*. (Paris, 1938.)

INDEX OF ARTISTS

THE PLATES

E

I CARLE VERNET: The Palais Royal in about 1810

II DESFRICHES: A Landscape

III   HUBERT ROBERT: Ruins

IV HUBERT ROBERT: Steps in a Garden

V   BOUCHER: A Landscape

VI MARÉCHAL: La Terrasse des Tuileries

VII   MEUNIER: Les Guichets du Louvre

VIII   JEAN-BAPTISTE OUDRY: Miroir d'Eau dans les Jardins d'Arcueil

IX LE PRINCE: La Danse russe

X ANTOINE WATTEAU: Moïse sauvé des Eaux

XI FRAGONARD: La Grande Allée de Cypres de la Villa d'Este à Tivoli

XII   DESPREZ: The Illumination of the Cross in Saint Peter's at Rome

XIII   MOREAU L'AÎNÉ: La Maison du Jardinier

XIV   VALENCIENNES: A View of Rome

XV   LAVREINCE: La Redoute Chinoise

XVI DESRAIS: La Promenade du Jardin du Palais Royal

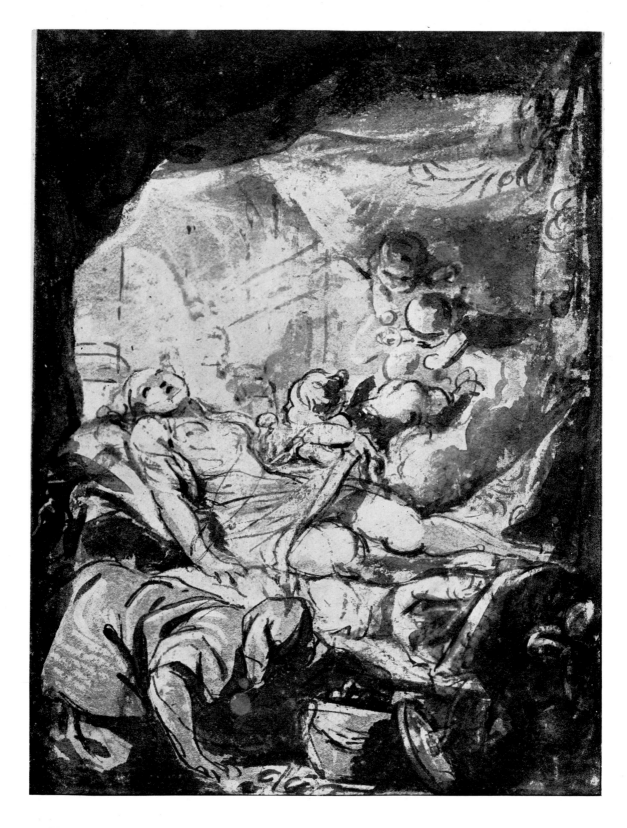

XVII DESHAYS DE COLLEVILLE: Danaë

XVIII   TRINQUESSE: Portrait of a young Woman Artist

XIX GREUZE: Portrait, said to be of the Duc d'Orléans, father of Philippe Egalité

XX   FRAGONARD: The Abbé de Saint Non

XXI CHANTEREAU: A Boy seated

XXII FRANÇOIS CASANOVA: A Cavalry Man

XXIII   JEAURAT: A Man reading

XXIV FRAGONARD: La Confidence

XXV   LAVREINCE: La Promenade

XXVI CARMONTELLE: Diderot and Grimm

XXVII   MERCIER: A Lady asleep

XXVIII   PATER: A seated Woman

XXIX   EISEN: Scene in a Ballroom

XXX   BOUCHER: A Reading in the Salon of Mme Geoffrin, at 372 Rue Saint-Honoré

XXXI   MOREAU LE JEUNE: Mme du Barry recevant à souper Louis XV à Louveciennes,
le 2 Septembre 1771

XXXII PIERRE-ALEXANDRE WILLE (?): A Performance at the Opéra Comique

XXXIII   DEMACHY: A Picture Sale

XXXIV   MOREAU LE JEUNE: Souper dans La Salle de l'Opéra à Versailles

XXXV   LAJOUE: L'Assemblée au Salon

XXXVI   FRANÇOIS LEMOYNE: Study for a Painting for a Ceiling

XXXVII   LA TOUR: Portrait of Crébillon

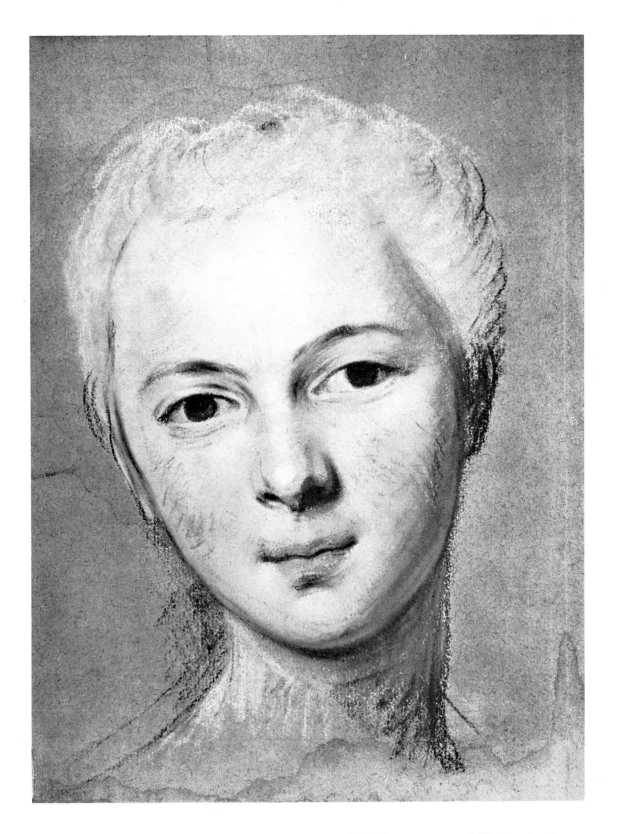

XXXVIII   LA TOUR: Mlle Puvigné

XXXIX DANLOUX: Mme de Pressigny and her mother, Mme Digneron

XL   DAVID: Portraits of Alexandre Lenoir and his wife, Adélaide Binard

XLI ANTOINE COYPEL: Study of a Girl's Head

XLII   CHARLES NICOLAS COCHIN: Portrait of the Comte de Caylus

A. Coipel.

XLIII   ANTOINE COYPEL: Head of a Satyr

XLIV   BOUCHER: Venus and Cupid

XLV GABRIEL DE SAINT-AUBIN: A Self-portrait and other Studies

XLVI ELISABETH-LOUISE VIGÉE-LEBRUN: Head of a young Girl

XLVII BOCQUET: A Costume Study—a Chinaman dancing

XLVIII DAVID: A Study for 'Le Sacre': Napoleon crowning himself

XLIX CHARDIN: La Vinaigrette, Louis XV

L CHARDIN: Scene at an Inn

LI LANCRET: Studies for 'Le Déjeuner au Jambon'

LII DURAMEAU: The Card Party

LIII FRAGONARD: Le Verrou

LIV   BAUDOUIN: Le Fruit de l'Amour secret

LV PORTAIL: Le Duo

LVI   VINCENT: The Painter Hall and his Wife, née Gobin

la peste des ardens, qui se manifesta à Paris l'an 1190,
Première composition du tableau de Doyen, quel on
voit à Paris dans l'Eglise F. Roch.

LVII   DOYEN: A Study for 'Le Miracle des Ardents ou Sainte Geneviève des Ardents'

LVIII   CHARLES NATOIRE: Interior of the French Académie in Rome

LIX DESPORTES: A Self-portrait

LX   PRUD'HON: Josephine

LXI GILLOT: La Mort de Maître André

LXII GABRIEL DE SAINT-AUBIN: Réunion sous les Orangers

LXIII LAGRENÉE: The Painter in his Studio

NOTES ON THE PLATES

Measurements are given in millimetres

Frontispiece
DUGOURC, Jean Démosthène (1749–1805)
A GARDEN SCENE
Gouache
330 : 450
Exh: London, Messrs Wildenstein: 'French Paintings and Drawings', 1946 (16).
A minor artist known principally as a draughtsman of architecture and industrial art; he designed décors for the Opera and designs for silk for the Manufacturers of Lyons.
London, Peter Gregory, Esq.

Colour plate, facing page 23
WATTEAU, Antoine (1684-1721)
A WOMAN AT HER TOILET
Black and red chalks
341 : 221
Inscr: *Watteau* in Julienne's hand below to left.
Coll: Ottley (Lugt, 2664); Lawrence (Lugt 2445); Woodburn.
Lit: G. Lafenestre: *Dessins de Watteau*, Paris 1907, Pl. 79.
Uzanne: *Drawings of Watteau*, London 1908, Pl. XII; Edmond de Goncourt: *Catalogue raisonné de l'Oeuvre peint, dessiné et gravé d'Antoine Watteau*, Paris 1875, Pl. 349, No. 13, describes it as the original of the etching by Boucher in the Bibliothèque de l'Arsenal, G. 458.
K. T. Parker: 'The drawings by Antoine Watteau in the British Museum', *Old Master Drawings*, Vol. V, June 1930, No. 49; K. T. Parker: *The Drawings of Antoine Watteau*, London 1932, Pl. 83.
A similar drawing was in the Walter Gay Collection, Paris (Repr. K. T. Parker, *op. cit.* Pl. 87).
London, British Museum.

I. VERNET, Antoine-Charles-Horace, *called* CARLE (1758–1836)
THE PALAIS ROYAL IN ABOUT 1810
Pen and bistre wash
309 : 262
Signed: *Carl Vernet*
Exh: Paris, Musée Carnavalet: 'Trois Siècles de Dessin parisien', 1946 (367).
Paris, Musée Carnavalet.

II. DESFRICHES, Thomas Aignan (1715–1800)
A LANDSCAPE
Plumbago
380 : 250
Coll: Henri Cadet de Limay, 1864.
Lit: Ratouis de Limay: *Aignan-Thomas Desfriches (1715–1800)*, Paris 1907, p. 187.
Chateauroux, Musée.

III. ROBERT, Hubert (1733–1808)
RUINS
Red chalk
363 : 283
Rotterdam, Boyman Museum.

IV. ROBERT, Hubert
STEPS IN A GARDEN
Red chalk
445 : 325
Coll: Richard Owen.
Exh: Fogg Art Museum: 'French Drawings and prints of the Eighteenth Century', 1934 (24); Buffalo, Albright Art Gallery: 'Master Drawings', 1935 (86 : Repr.).
Lit: Agnes Mongan: *French Drawings and Prints of the Eighteenth Century. Bulletin of the Fogg Art Museum*, Vol. III, No. 2, (1934) p. 8, No. 4.
This is presumably a view in one of the Italian villas in which Hubert Robert worked.
Providence, Rhode Island. J. N. Brown, Esq.

V. BOUCHER, François (1703–1770)
A LANDSCAPE
Black chalk heightened with white on grey brown paper
265 : 490
Carries a false signature: f. B.
Coll: Amckarsward No. 66.
Lit: Schönbrunner—Meder, Vol. VII, p. 14 (Plate); *Collection de Dessins du Musée National de Stockholm*: François Boucher. Preface d'Axel Gauffin. Introd. et cat. Ragnar Hoppe, Malmö 1928, No. XXXIX.
Stockholm, National Museum

VI. MARÉCHAL, Laurent-Charles (*op.* 1778–1789)
LA TERRASSE DES TUILERIES
Watercolour
244 : 305
Signed and dated: *Maréchal an* 1786
Exh: Paris, Musée Carnavalet: 'Trois Siècles de Dessin Parisien', 1946 (228).
Paris, Musée Carnavalet.

VII. MEUNIER, Philippe, died 1734
LES GUICHETS DU LOUVRE
Pencil heightened with watercolour
180 : 260
Signed on the right: *Meunier*
Coll: Defer-Dumesnil, 1900 (No. 194), bought 4.000 frcs. by Muhlbacher; Muhlbacher, 1907; P. Decourcelle, 1911.
Exh: Paris, Musée Carnavalet: 'La Vie parisienne au XVIIIe Siècle', 1928 (207).
Shown in the drawing is the Stall of Blaisot, the print dealer.
A signed drawing by Meunier of the Palais Royal is also in the Musée Carnavalet: Views of the Eglise Sainte Geneviève, 1788, and of the Château de Saint Cloud, 1783, both of which are engraved, were also in the Defer-Dumesnil Collection.
Paris, private collection.

VIII. OUDRY, Jean-Baptiste (1686–1755)
MIROIR D'EAU DANS LES JARDINS D'ARCUEIL
Black chalk heightened with chalk on blue paper
308 : 467
Signed and dated in pen: *J. B. Oudry* 1744
Coll: Armand Valton.
Exh: Paris, Petit Palais: 'Paysage français', 1925 (625); Ecole des Beaux-Arts: 'Art français des XVIIe et XVIIIe Siècles', 1933 (10); Copenhagen: 'Art français du XVIIIe Siècle', 1935 (465).
Lit: J. Locquin: *Catalogue de l'Oeuvre de J. B. Oudry*, No. 651; Marcheix: 'Les Nouveaux Dessins de l'Ecole des Beaux-Arts' in *Arts et les Artistes*, VIII, 1909, p. 263; Repr. L. Hourticq, E. Dacier et G. Brière: *Le Paysage français de Poussin à Corot*, Paris, Pl. XXXI; P. Lavallée: *Dessins français du XVIIIe Siècle*, p. 28, Pl. XIV.
Pierre Lavallée, in his admirable notice on this drawing, mentions the influence of the Dutch artists of the seventeenth century on Oudry, who in an unpublished manuscript in the Ecole des Beaux-Arts (M.S. No. 205) spoke of the impression made on him by Berchem.

The figures in the drawing were added at the end of the eighteenth or beginning of the nineteenth century. According to Edmond de Goncourt (*La Maison d'un Artiste*, I, p. 30), they were put in by a dealer who owned a number of such drawings and thought to facilitate their sale by adding figures to 'Faire peupler leur vide et leur solitude par un artiste contemporain'. These figures have been attributed to Moreau le jeune, and to Boilly.
Paris, Ecole des Beaux-Arts.

IX. LE PRINCE, Jean-Baptiste (1734–1781)
LA DANSE RUSSE
Brush and indian ink over preliminary work in red and black chalk
325 : 566
Coll: Edmond de Goncourt (176); S. S. Bond (Sale, Christie's, 9.6.1944 (66).
Exh: Paris, Ecole des Beaux-Arts: 'Dessins des Maîtres anciens', 1879 (610); London, Burlington House: French Exhibition, 1932 (825 : 708).*
The composition is believed to correspond to the left-hand portion of a picture sold with the collection of the Duchesse de Raguse in 1857 (35), and should also be compared with Le Prince's aquatint, dated 1769, entitled *La danse russe* (Hedou, 137).
London, private collection.

X. WATTEAU, Antoine
MOÏSE SAUVÉ DES EAUX
Red chalk
214 : 303
Coll: Jules Boilly Sale (Paris, March 19th, 1869, No. 225); Armand Valton.
Exh: London, Burlington House: French Exhibition, 1932 (744 : 785); Paris, Ecole des Beaux-Arts: 'L'Art français du XVIIIe Siècle', 1933 (163); Paris, Galerie des Beaux-Arts: 'Le Dessin français dans les Collections français du XVIIIe Siècle', 1935 (10); Copenhagen: 'L'Art français au XVIIIe Siècle', 1935 (536).
Lit: E. Dacier: *Dessins de Maîtres français, I*, 'Antoine Watteau', Paris 1930 (44); P. Lavallée: *Trésors des Bibliothèques de France*, Vol. 1, p. 160; *Les Dessins français du XVIIIe Siècle à l'Ecole*

---

* The two different numbers in references to the French Exhibition at Burlington House, London, in 1932 refer respectively to the ordinary and the commemorative catalogue of the Exhibition.

des Beaux-Arts, Paris 1928, Pl. 5; K. T. Parker, *The Drawings of Antoine Watteau*, London 1932, Pl. 24.

Engraved on wood by Jules Germain.

Almost certainly one of the drawings executed by Antoine Watteau after the latter's Italian drawings, during his stay with Crozat. According to K. T. Parker: *The Drawings of Antoine Watteau*, pp. 25 and 43, it is a drawing after a study by Veronese once in the Buttolier Lasquin Collection.

A project for Watteau's 'Morceau de Reception à l'Académie Royale', which was not finally carried out and of which this is the only remaining document. One of Watteau's rare compositional drawings.

Paris, Ecole des Beaux-Arts.

XI. FRAGONARD, Jean Honoré (1732–1806)
LA GRANDE ALLÉE DE CYPRES DE LA VILLA D'ESTE À TIVOLI
Bistre wash
460 : 340
Signed: *Fragonard* and inscribed: *Vue de la Villa d'Este à Tivoli.*

Exh: Paris, Galerie J. Seligmann: 'Dessins de Fragonard', 1931 (82); London, Burlington House: French Exhibition, 1932 (1015: 676) Pl. CLXXV; Paris: 'Chefs d'Oeuvre de l'Art français', 1937 (532).

Lit: J. Meder: *Handzeichnungen französischer Meister in der Albertina*, Vienna 1922, p. 31. Probably drawn about 1760, during the artist's first visit to Italy. A large sanguine drawing in the Musée de Besançon (Paris collection) shows the same composition, and was probably executed immediately before this. The Villa d'Este and its gardens were frequently drawn by Fragonard.

Vienna, Albertina.

XII. DESPREZ, Louis Jean (1743–1804)
THE ILLUMINATION OF THE CROSS IN SAINT PETER'S AT ROME
Watercolour
148 : 107

Coll: Mme Ingres, part of an album which also contained Desprez' drawing of 'Les Jardins de la Villa Médici, Rome'.
Lit: M. G. Wollin: *Gravures originales de Desprez ou exécutées d'après ses Dessins*, Malmö 1933, pp. 109–110; *Desprez en Italie*, Malmö 1939, p. 156, Fig. 201.

Guiffrey—Marcel, Vol. V, No. 3642.

This is probably the drawing sent by Desprez to the Académie Royale d'Architecture, when he was presented by Perronet on November 12th, 1782. Later engraved with some modifications by Francesco Piranesi (1787), and the watercolour of the print was made by Desprez himself, as well as an etching which is in the National Museum, Stockholm. The sketch for the latter work is not by Desprez but by an artist near to him, and may be compared with another drawing of the interior of Saint Peter's in the Musée de Besançon (102), attributed by Mlle J. Magnin to Challes or Clerisseau: *Les Dessins du XVIIIe Siècle au Musée de Besançon* (Besançon 1919).

Another drawing, a gouache similar in style, was in the possession of Guiraud. Another version seems to have passed through the C. Morin Sale, Paris 1924.

The same subject seen from about the same angle was represented by D. Louis and is also in the Louvre, with figures by J. F. Amand: Guiffrey—Marcel, Vol. I, No. 40.

Paris, Musée du Louvre.

XIII. MOREAU, Louis-Gabriel, L'Aîné (1740–1806)
LA MAISON DU JARDINIER
Gouache
445 : 451
Signed and dated at the bottom left-hand corner: *L. M.* (1786)

Coll: Abbé d'Auberive who bought it from the uncle of Mme Henry Fritsch-Estrangin.
Exh: Paris: Galerie Charpentier: 'Hubert Robert, Louis Moreau', 1922 (105).
Lit: Georges Wildenstein: *Louis Moreau, l'Aîné*, Paris 1923, No. 46, Pl. 22.

Paris, private collection.

XIV. VALENCIENNES, Pierre-Henri (1750–1819)
A VIEW OF ROME
Pencil and wash
260 : 390

Coll: Victor Loutrel
Of Rome, Valenciennes wrote: 'The city of Rome offers great interest to a landscapist . . . because of the charming buildings which decorate the world's capital. Their individuality increases their picturesqueness . . . the mingling of Ancient and Modern; the combination of irregularity and

symmetry, of incoherence and harmony, of folly and reason, form a whole which is original and it is found only in Italy—particularly in Rome. Besides, many convents with few windows and large uninterrupted surfaces produce a calm and spacious effect, which further augments the severity of style, in its restfulness to the eyes. . . . All these buildings, sometimes in harmony, sometimes in contrast, but always united in a noble manner, constitute the whole which gives the principal cities of Italy their original physiognomy. The hot climate of Rome produces a vigorous colour in the vegetation not to be found in Northern climates; the earth is of a warmer hue; the rocks show up in a stronger relief; the greens are darker and more varied; the sky bluer; the clouds more vibrant and colourful.' *Elements*, pp. 595–6, cited by Lionello Venturi, 'Pierre-Henri de Valenciennes', *The Art Quarterly*, Vol. IV, 1941, pp. 89–109.

Havre, Musée.

XV. LAVREINCE, Niklas, *called* LAFRENSEN (1737–1807)
LA REDOUTE CHINOISE
Gouache
295 : 370

Exh: Paris, Musée des Arts Décoratifs: 'L'Art suédois depuis le Moyen-Age jusqu'en 1880', 1929 (107).
This interesting drawing represents a fête in a Parisian Vauxhall decorated in the Chinese fashion.

Östergötland, Museum of Art and Archaeology.

XVI. DESRAIS, Claude Louis (1746–1816)
LA PROMENADE DU JARDIN DU PALAIS ROYAL
Pen and sepia wash
290 : 356

Exh: Paris, Musée Carnavalet: 'Paris au XVIIIe Siècle', 1934 (5).
Engr: Le Cœur. This print which is in the same direction was long attributed to Debucourt, and is the pendant of 'Promenade de la Galerie du Palais Royal'. M. Fenaille-Vaucaire: *L'Oeuvre gravé de Debucourt*, Paris 1899, p. 12.

Paris, Musée Carnavalet.

XVII. DESHAYS de COLLEVILLE, Jean-Baptiste-Henri, *called* LE ROMAIN (1729–1765)
DANAË

Pen and bistre wash, heightened with white chalk on grey paper
223 : 168
Inscr. on the mount on the right: *Deshays*
Lit: Guiffrey—Marcel, Vol. V, No. 3624.
A pupil of Restout and Van Loo and the son-in-law of Boucher, which in a large measure explains his style.

Paris, Musée du Louvre.

XVIII. TRINQUESSE, Louis-René (*circa* 1746–*circa* 1800)
PORTRAIT OF A YOUNG WOMAN ARTIST
Black chalk touched up with white on blue paper
350 : 260

Signed and dated on bottom right: *Trinquesse f à Orléans en* 1785
Exh: Paris, Orangerie: 'Chefs d'Oeuvre des Musées de Provence', 1931 (114); Paris, Musée Carnavalet: 'Chefs d'Oeuvres des Musées de Provence', 1933 (185); Copenhagen: 'L'Art français au XVIIIe Siècle', 1935 (519).

Orléans, Musée.

XIX. GREUZE, Jean Baptiste (1725–1805)
PORTRAIT, SAID TO BE OF THE DUC D'ORLÉANS, FATHER OF PHILIPPE ÉGALITÉ
Sanguine and black stone
519 : 326
Inv: 27005

Coll: Paignon-Dijonval, No. 3691; Defer, 1842.
Exh: Paris, Musée Galliéra, 'Exposition du Costume', 1937.
Lit: Reiset. *Notice des Dessins exposés au Musée du Louvre*, Deuxième Partie, Paris 1869, No. 769. J.-M. C. Martin: *Catalogue raisonné de l'Oeuvre peint et dessiné de Greuze*, No. 1268; Guiffrey-Marcel, Vol. VI, No. 4568; E. J. de Goncourt: *L'Art du XVIIIe Siécle*, 1882, p. 83; J. Bouchot-Saupique: *Quartorze Dessins de J. B. Greuze.* Collection de reproductions de dessins publiés sous la direction de Gabriel Rouchès, VII, Paris 1939, No. 13.
Engr: Jules de Goncourt.

Paris, Musée du Louvre.

XX. FRAGONARD, Jean Honoré
THE ABBÉ DE SAINT NON
Red chalk
473 : 378

Coll: Xavier Atger.
The Abbé J. C. Richard de Saint Non (1727–

1791) was an amateur artist of talent. His friendship with Fragonard is celebrated and was valuable to both. Fragonard drew and painted many portraits of his friend, one of the most notable of which is in the Lacaze collection, in the Louvre. See L. Guimbaud: 'Saint Non et Fragonard', Paris 1928.

Montpellier, Musée Atger.

XXI. CHANTEREAU, Jérôme François (d. 1757)
A BOY SEATED
Red and black chalk heightened with white on grey-brown paper
203 : 132
Coll: Crozat; Tessin (2810).
Lit: Robert Rey: *Quelques Satellites de Watteau*, Paris 1931, p. 177.
Stockholm, National Museum

XXII. CASANOVA, François (1727–1802)
A CAVALRY MAN
Black chalk and bistre wash
518 : 338
Lit: F. Reiset: No. 676; Guiffrey-Marcel, Vol. III, No. 2155.
RF 25147.
'En ses dessins, il a un peu de la furia que mettait le Bourguignon dans sa peinture militaire.' E. de Goncourt.
Paris, Musée du Louvre

XXIII. JEAURAT, Etienne (1699–1789)
A MAN READING
Red chalk and grey watercolour wash
426 : 297
Signed: *E. Jeaurat* 1769 in left lower corner
Coll: Orléans (not in Lugt: resembling No. 2781, but surmounted by a crown).
Exh: London, Messrs. Colnaghi: 'Exhibition of Old Master Drawings', 1936 (22. Repr.).
Lit: K. T. Parker: *Catalogue of the Drawings in the Ashmolean Museum, Oxford.* Oxford 1938, Vol. I, No. 516, Pl. LXXVI, p. 252.
As K. T. Parker has pointed out, the statuesque pose of the figure and the large scale on which it is drawn show analogies to the Chinaman in the Albertina, which was formerly attributed to Watteau but is demonstrably by Jeaurat (see *Old Master Drawings*, Vol. V, 1930, p. 52, Pl.

XXXIII). Two other drawings also in the Albertina and formerly thought to be by Chardin are plausibly attributed to Jeaurat by Jacques Mathey (see *Old Master Drawings*, Vol. VIII, 1933, pp. 8–10). Their execution is lighter and more diffuse in style.
On the reverse is a large study of a woman's head in classical style, drawn in red chalk, which is clearly from a plaster cast.
Oxford, Ashmolean Museum.

XXIV. FRAGONARD, Jean Honoré
LA CONFIDENCE
Sepia wash on a plumbago preparation
280 : 208
Coll: The provenance of this drawing was not known until Marius Paulme discovered it at the end of 1925: he believed that it was the 'Confidence, Dessin lavé au Bistre' in Baron Brunet-Denons Sale, Paris, 1846, No. 264.
Marius Paulme (Sale, Paris 1929, Part I, 86, Pl. 58), 560,000 Frcs; F. Koenigs, Harlem.
Exh: Paris: 'Exposition Fragonard', 1931; Rotterdam, Boymans Museum, 1934–35 (58, Pl. XXVII); Paris: 'Chefs d'Oeuvre de l'Art français', 1937 (541 : Album, Pl. 95).
Lit: C. F. Förster: *Sammlung Franz Koenigs französischer Meister von XVIII Jahrhundert*, Frankfurt-am-Main, 1930, Pl. 18.
It is the exact pendant to 'La Lecture' in the Louvre (26651). The two sitters are believed to be Mme Fragonard and her sister Mlle Gérard.
Rotterdam, Boymans Museum.

XXV. LAVREINCE, Niklas, *called* LAFRENSEN
LA PROMENADE
Gouache
410 : 310
Exh: Paris, Musée Carnavalet: 'Les Salons Littéraires', 1923 (279).
The figures represented are the Duchesse de Bourbon, the Duchesse de Luynes et de Chevreuse and the Vicomtesse de Laval.
This drawing is very different from Lavreince's usual work, which may be related to two pendants once in the Audonin Collection and later the Muhlbacher Collection, 'Les Graces parisiennes au Bois de Vincennes' and the 'Trois Soeurs du Parc de Saint-Cloud'.
Paris, private collection.

XXVI. CARMONTELLE, Louis called CARROGIS (1717–1806)

DIDEROT AND GRIMM

Coloured chalks and touches of watercolour

285 : 180

Inscr. on the reverse of the mount: M. Diderot avec son ami M. Grimm par Carmontelle en 1761. Also a manuscript note in the hand of Mme de Vandeul, Diderot's grand-daughter through marriage: Dessin demeuré toujours dans ma famille; ma grand'mère, née de Vandeul, étant la petite fille de Mme de Vandeul, fille de Diderot.

The drawing has been enlarged by Carmontelle on the left and at the top.

Dated: 1761.

Coll: Vandeul family.

Exh: Copenhagen, 'L'Art français au XVIIIe Siècle', 1935 (327); Paris, Palais National des Arts: 'Chefs d'Oeuvre de l'Art français', 1937 (518).

According to tradition, Carmontelle executed three versions of the composition; two of these he gave to Mme D'Epinay who, keeping one, presented the other to Mme de Vandeul, Diderot's daughter. One drawing, dated 1760 on the reverse, which was later in the possession of a Parisian collector, was exhibited in the Carmontelle Exhibition at the Musée Carnavalet, Paris, 1933 (14).

Paris, private collection

XXVII. MERCIER, Philippe (1689–1760)

A LADY ASLEEP

Red chalk and pencil

228 : 260

Coll: J. C. Robinson (the mark is now erased).

With certain derivations, it resembles the figure on the right of 'L'heureuse Rencontre' (otherwise 'La Promenade') formerly ascribed to Watteau but shown by an etching inscribed *P. Mercier Pinxit et sculp* to be by Mercier. The painting, which was formerly in the collection of M. Marcel Bernstein and now belongs to M. Wildenstein, is in reverse to the print. The drawing is one of a set of four formerly in the collection of Sir J. C. Robinson. One of these went via the Malcom collection to the British Museum. Another which has not yet been found is an exact preliminary study for the girl seated on the ground in the right middle distance of the picture. See K. T. Parker:

Mercier, Angélis and De Bar, Old Master Drawings, Vol. VII, December 1932, pp. 36–40, Fig. 5, and Pls. 42, 43, 44.

Another related drawing is in the Cottonion Collection, Plymouth. See Denys Sutton: *Old Master Drawings*, Vol. XII, June 1938, p. 14, Pl. 13. Yet another related drawing was on the London art market in 1947.

Oxford, J. N. Bryson, Esq.

XXVIII. PATER, Jean-Baptiste Joseph (1695–1736)

A SEATED WOMAN

Red chalk with touches of black

265 : 296

Clearly a study for the principal figure in one of Pater's paintings which is not yet identified. It is similar to the figures in his 'L'Offre des Fleurs'. (Benjamin Stern Collection, New York). F. Ingersoll-Smouse, *J. B. Pater*, Paris. No. 56, Fig. 46 or the two versions of 'La Danse' in the Baron Lambert Collection, Bruxelles, No. 234, Fig. 56, and at Sans Souci No. 233, Fig. 58.

Manchester, private collection.

XXIX. EISEN, Charles (1720–1778)

SCENE IN A BALLROOM

Pen and bistre and indian ink with watercolours and touches of body colour (partly oxidised)

159 : 219

Signed, *S. E. Fecit*, in lower corner.

Coll: Saint.

Lit: K. T. Parker: *Catalogue of the Drawings in the Ashmolean Museum, Oxford.* Oxford 1938, p. 489 (Pl. LXXXII).

The provenance from the Saint collection being independently recorded, there can be little doubt that the drawing is identical with No. 11 in the Saint Sale, 1846. This is, however, attributed to Cochin and listed as such by the Goncourts in their *'Art du XVIIIe Siècle'*, Vol. 11, p. 384. The Goncourts had probably not seen the drawings themselves and were therefore unaware of the signature; Saint's attribution can only be explained by assuming that he read the second letter (which is ambiguous) as F for example, C(ochin) F(ils), Fecit. Ostensibly, however, the letter is E and the style accords well with Eisen's work, such as the signed 'Allegory' in the Städel Museum, Frankfurt-am-Main (Repr. *Stift und Feder*, 1926, Pl. 23) and the signed design for a vignette now in the Morgan Library, New

York (Repr. *Fairfax Murray Publication*, Part III, Pl. 111). Other drawings by the same hand are in the Berlin Print Room and in the British Museum.

Oxford, Ashmolean Museum.

XXX. BOUCHER, François

A READING IN THE SALON OF MME GEOFFRIN, AT 372 RUE SAINT-HONORÉ
Black chalk, touched up with white on blue paper
310 : 460

Coll: J. Echorcheville

Exh: Paris, Musée Carnavalet: 'Les Grands Salons Littéraires', 1927 (144); Paris, Galerie des Beaux-Arts: 'Le Siècle de Louis XV vu par les Artistes', 1934 (154); Paris, Musée Galliera: 'Huit Siècle de la Vie britannique à Paris', 1948 (212). Served as a model for a painting, with some variants, by Gabriel Lemonnier in the Académie des Arts at Rouen, which was engraved by Debucourt and Jazet in 1831.

The figures in the drawing include d'Alembert, the 'philosophe', who is reading a manuscript; on his right are Mme Geoffrin, beside whom are seated the Prince de Conti on the right and Fontenelle on the left.

Another artist of the period, Hubert Robert, made several paintings and drawings of Mme Geoffrin in her cabinet and bedroom (*cf.* the two drawings in the Valence Museum, exhibited in Paris, 1937, 'Chefs d'Oeuvre de l'Art français', (570–571) which are studies for two paintings in a Paris private collection.

Paris, private collection

XXXI. MOREAU, Jean-Michel, Le Jeune (1741–1814)

MME DU BARRY RECEVANT À SOUPER LOUIS XV À LOUVECIENNES, LE 2 SEPTEMBRE 1771
Pen and ink and watercolour
315 : 263

Signed at the bottom: *J. M. Moreau Le Jeune*, 1771.

At the foot of the drawing (now attached to the back of the mount) is the inscription: *Feste donnée à Louveciennes le 2 Septembre* 1771, divided by two coats of arms, of which one is that of Mme Du Barry.

Exh: London, Burlington House: French Exhibition, 1932 (710 : 824); Paris, Galerie des Beaux-

Arts: 'Le Siècle de Louis XV vu par les Artistes' (34); Copenhagen: 'L'Art Français au XVIIIe Siècle', 1935 (449).

Lit: Guiffrey—Marcel, Vol. VI, No. 360; G. Scheffer: *Moreau Le Jeune*. Paris 1915. Repr. p. 2.

Paris, Musée du Louvre.

XXXII. WILLE, Pierre-Alexandre (1748–1821), attributed to.

A PERFORMANCE AT THE OPÉRA COMIQUE
Watercolour
313 : 252

Exh: Paris, Musée Carnavalet: 'Le Théatre à Paris aux XVIIe et XVIIIe Siècles', 1929 (210). The play is performed in the old Hôtel de Bourgogne in the rue Mauconseil.

Paris, Bibliothèque de l'Opéra.

XXXIII. DEMACHY, Pierre Antoine (1723–1807)

A PICTURE SALE
Pen, heightened with bistre wash and chinese ink
266 : 321

Lit: Les Dessins de la Collection Léon Bonnat au Musée de Bayonne (2ème année), 1925, No. 49, where it is attributed to Gabriel de Saint-Aubin. E. Dacier: *Gabriel de Saint-Aubin*, Paris-Bruxelles 1931, 2 vols. Nos. 811, p. 146.

M. Dacier, who points out that an attribution to Saint-Aubin is not to be sustained, suggests the name of Demachy which is substantiated by comparison with the artist's signed 'Le Marchand d'Orvietans sur le Pont Neuf à Paris', formerly in the Marius Paulme Collection (Sale, Paris 1929, No. 61, Pl. 42).

A drawing of a Sale by Saint-Aubin is in the D. David-Weill Collection: E. Dacier, *op. cit.* No. 808.

Bayonne, Musée Bonnat.

XXXIV. MOREAU, Jean-Michel, Le Jeune

SOUPER DANS LA SALLE DE L'OPÉRA À VERSAILLES 16 MAI 1770
Sepia and pen
230 : 263

The drawing carries the signatures: *Bon L. D. D.* (*Le Duc d'Aumont, premier Gentilhomme de la Chambre*) *et avetté pour être exécuté. De la Ferté* (*Papillon de la Ferté, intendant des Menus Plaisirs*).

Coll: Doucet (Sale, 5.7.1912, 36 bis, S. Bardac).

Exh: Paris, Orangerie, 'L'Art de Versailles', 1932 (102).

Lit: E. Dacier (attributed to Slodtz): *Société de Reproductions des Dessins de Maîtres*, 3e Année 1911.

Like the 'Bal Paré', was designed as an engraving. Moreau received 2,000 louis for this drawing in 1774. It was praised by the Duc d'Aumont and the Intendant des Menus Plaisirs. It was formerly attributed to Slodtz, but was restored to Moreau by A. Vuaflart in the Bardac Sale Catalogue. The Banquet was given on the marriage day of Louis XVI in the Salle of the Opéra which had been built by Gabriel and exists to this day.

Paris, private collection.

XXXV. LAJOUE, Jacques (1687–1761)
L'ASSEMBLÉE AU SALON
Pen and wash
377 : 235

Coll: Doistau.

Exh: Paris, Musée des Arts Decoratifs: 'Le Siège français du Moyen-Age à nos Jours', 1947 (365). One of the most effective drawings by this artist, who generally represents groups or figures taken from Watteau on a rococo staircase. He died too late, at the time of the return to the antique, 'méprisé et sans occupation' (Mariette).

Paris, private collection.

XXXVI. LEMOYNE, François (1688–1737)
STUDY FOR A PAINTING FOR A CEILING
Pen, wash and white chalk on blue paper
373 : 542
Nos. 30, 596
Paris, Musée du Louvre.

XXXVII. LA TOUR, Maurice QUENTIN de (1704–1788)
PORTRAIT OF CRÉBILLON
Pastel preparation
240 : 310

Coll: De La Tour, Musée de Saint-Quentin, No. 44.

Lit: D. Diderot: *Salon*, 1761; H. Erhard, *La Tour der Pastellmaler Ludwigs* XV, 1918, p. 44, Pl. 44; A. Besnard and Georges Wildenstein: *La Tour*, Paris 1928, No. 80.

A preparation for the pastel exhibited in the Salon of 1761 which shows Crébillon in antique costume and with a bare head without a wig. Described by Denis Diderot in his 'Salon' of 1761, p. 130,

and drawn and mentioned by Gabriel de Saint-Aubin in his *Livret du Salon* of 1761.

E. Dacier: *Gabriel de Saint-Aubin*, 5. VI. p. 14.

A drawing of Crébillon by La Tour was in the Quintin Crauford Sale (Paris 1820, 375), and the M.A. Sale (3.11.1847, Wildenstein, No. 81). A three-quarters bust of Crébillon is also listed by Wildenstein, No. 82.

Saint-Quentin, Musée.

XXXVIII. LA TOUR, Maurice QUENTIN de
MLLE PUVIGNÉ
Pastel preparation
240 : 320

Lit: E. Fleury, G. Brière: *Catalogue des Pastels de la M. Q. La Tour Collection*, Musée de Saint-Quentin et Musée du Louvre, Paris 1920, No. 39; H. Erhard: *La Tour der Pastellmaler Ludwigs* XV, 1918, p. 73, Pl. 73.
A. Besnard and Georges Wildenstein: *La Tour*, Paris 1928, Fig. 202.

An oval pastel of Mlle Puvigné was in the Brandon Sale (New York, 1907, 66), and an oil portrait in the Anderdelyn Sale (London 1926, 50).

Mlle Puvigné (1736–1783) was a dancer of the period. Drawings of her by Bocquet are in the Bibliothèque de l'Opéra.

Saint-Quentin, Musée.

XXXIX. DANLOUX, Henri Pierre (1753–1809)
MME DE PRESSIGNY AND HER MOTHER, MME DIGNERON
Chinese ink

The measurements of this drawing are not now available.

Lit: Baron Robert Portalis: *Henri-Pierre Danloux, Peintre de Portraits, et son Journal pendant l'Emigration* (1753–1809). Paris 1910, p. 256.

The circumstances attendant upon the execution of this drawing are known. Mme de Pressigny was the daughter of M and Mme Digneron, leading members of the rich colonial society of Saint-Domingo and Martinique resident in London during the French Revolution. Her marriage to M Gilbert de Pressigny took place after lengthy negotiations with her father. After her daughter's marriage, Mme Digneron decided to have her portrait, surrounded by her children, painted by Danloux. On July 18th, 1795, Danloux made a preparatory sketch and sittings continued throughout August. The portrait, however, was not to be completed. Mme de Pressigny was a determined woman. She quarrelled with her mother because she continued to receive a certain Mme de Belloy of whom she disapproved. Mme Danloux, the wife of the painter, was the recipient of the mother's complaints about Mme de Pressigny and her other daughter, Mme d'Osmond, who had not visited her for three weeks when she was ill. They all went to call on the mother who received Mme de Pressigny coldly in the painter's studio. Mme d'Osmond as a result told the painter not to place too much affection in his portrait of the mother as she no longer desired it. As a result the canvas which Mme Digneron had commissioned from the painter—four figures for 180 gns—remained unfinished except for the preliminary sketches, of which this drawing is one.

Mme de Pressigny remained in England until 1800, when she returned to France. During her stay in London, Danloux made another portrait of her on a small scale dressed as a peasant girl (*op. cit.*, p. 325). On another occasion, she and her sister (p. 316) took part in a drunken party at Greenwich which earned the disapproval of the Danloux (p. 328); on another occasion her husband was in tears on account of his wife's unkindness (p. 316). A portrait of 'Mme Digneron and her daughter embracing' attributed to Danloux was in the Pierquin Collection (p. 253).

Paris, private collection.

XL. DAVID, Jacques-Louis (1748–1825)
PORTRAITS OF ALEXANDRE LENOIR AND HIS WIFE, ADÉLAIDE BINARD
Black chalk and plumbago
165 : 215
Each drawing signed at the bottom: *L. David f.* 1809
Coll: Lenoir
Exh: Paris, Petit Palais: 'David et ses Elèves', 1913 (275); Petit Palais: 'Gros, ses amis, ses Elèves', 1936 (544); Zurich, Kunsthaus: 'Zeichnungen französischer Meister von David zu Millet', 1937 (65).
Lit: L'Art Vivant, 15.12.1925, p. 13; L. Cantinelli: *Jacques-Louis David*, Paris-Bruxelles 1930, Pl. LXVI; M. Serullaz: *Quatorze Dessins de J. L. David* (Collection de reproductions de dessins publiés sous la direction de Gabriel Rouches IX),

No. 10. A. Lenoir was Director of the Musée des Monuments français during the Revolution. See L. Courajod: *Le Journal d'Alexandre Lenoir et le Musée des Monuments français*, Paris 1878–1887.
Paris, Musée du Louvre.

XLI. COYPEL, Antoine (1661–1722)
STUDY OF A GIRL'S HEAD
Pastel on grey paper
150 : 155
Lit: F. Reiset, No. 698. Guiffrey—Marcel, Vol. IV, No. 3097.
Paris, Musée du Louvre.

XLII. COCHIN, Charles Nicolas (1715–1790)
PORTRAIT OF THE COMTE DE CAYLUS
Black stone
Diameter, 100
Inscr. on reverse: 'De Caylus, petit-neveu de Mme de Maintenon. Anne-Claude-Philippe de Tubière, comte de Caylus, naquit à Paris en 1692 et y mourut en 1765. Il commença par servir, mais, après la Paix de Rastadt, faite en 1714, il fit un voyage en Italie, puis passa dans le Levant, vit le fameux temple de Diane à Ephèse, etc. . . . Il s'est rendu très recommandable aux arts et aux sciences. Il le vois très souvent chez Mme Geoffrin qui a écrit ce qui précède.'
Coll: Mme Geoffrin (hung in her salon); Comte de la Bedoyère, Sale, Paris 1921 (42); Roquigny.
Exh: Paris, Musée Carnavalet: 'Les Grands Salons Littéraires', 1927 (116); Rouen, Musée, 'Exposition d'Art du XVIIIe Siècle, 1929, p. 165, Pl. 21.
Engr: Cochin, 1752.
One of a set of drawings by Cochin of prominent personalities of the period including David Hume, the Marquis de Marigny and Boucher.
Another portrait of Caylus in bust, profile to right, drawn and engraved by G. Dagoty, is in the Musée Carnavalet, Paris. It was exhibited in 'Le Dessin français dans les Collections du XVIIIe Siècle', Galerie des Beaux-Arts, Paris, 1935 (346). Cochin's celebrated drawing of the 'Concours pour le Prix Caylus, 1761', is now in the Louvre (S 1767), engraved by Flipart, 1763.
It was formerly in the Goncourt Collection.
Paris, private collection.

XLIII. COYPEL, Antoine

HEAD OF A SATYR

Red and black chalk heightened with white on brown paper

258 : 220

Inscr: *A Coipel*

Coll: Tessin (2857).

Exh: Stockholm, National Museum, 1922: 'Carl Gustaf Tessins Franska Handteckningar', (8); London, Burlington House: French Exhibition, 1932 (722 : 598); Paris, Galerie des Beaux-Arts: 'Le Dessin français dans les Collections du XVIIIe Siècle' (59); Paris, Palais National des Arts: 'Chefs d'Oeuvre de l'Art français', 1937 (525).

Lit: Schönbrunner—Meder, Vol. VI, No. 952.

Engr: J. Audran (Le Blanc, 100, Manuel de l'Amateur d'Estampes, Paris, 1854–1858).

This study was partly employed for 'Ariadne et Bacchus', and for 'Pan Elève de l'Amour'.

Stockholm, National Museum.

XLIV. BOUCHER, François

VENUS AND CUPID

Coloured chalk and pastel on grey paper

363 : 256

Signed and dated *f Boucher* 1759 in bottom left-hand corner

Coll: The collector's mark, which is said to be partly original, is signed with the letter G (the mark of Glomy), the eighteenth-century expert, frame maker and painter. (Lugt 1085, 1119); Marquis de Biron; Marius Paulme (Sale, Paris 1929, No. 26, Pl. XXI).

Earlier drawings by Boucher of 'Venus and Cupid' were in the Tabourier Collection Sale, Paris 1898, 119, dated 1748, in an Anonymous Sale, Paris 1906, and the V. Sardou Collection Sale, Paris 1909, dated 1752.

Providence, Rhode Island: J. N. Brown Esq.

XLV. SAINT-AUBIN, Gabriel Jacques de (1724–1780)

A SELF-PORTRAIT AND OTHER STUDIES

Watercolour

180 : 125

Inscr. in the hand of Augustin de Saint-Aubin: *Gabriel de Saint-Aubin*, and in the hand of the artist himself: *Mme la Marquise de Pompadour, morte le 15 Avril* 1764, beneath which 1764 is repeated.

Coll: Camille Groult; Anonymous Sale (Paris, 20 Novembre, 1942, 26).

Lit: E.-J. de Goncourt: *L'Art français du XVIIIe Siècle*, Paris; E. Dacier: *Gabriel de Saint-Aubin, Peintre, Graveur et Dessinateur*, Paris 1931, Vol. II, No. 1105.

This sketch occurs on page 2 of the *Livre de croquis*, a small volume in octavo (1,180 : 125) bound in clear brown calf, the spine of which is decorated with gilt and inscribed *Receuil*. It is dated 1760–1778.

A full description is given by M. Emile Dacier in *Le Livre de Croquis de Gabriel de Saint-Aubin*, Paris 1944.

For other self-portraits by Saint-Aubin see E. Dacier, *op. cit.* Nos. 22–237. The nearest is that in *Médaillon*, which may be dated 1764. E. Dacier, No. 232. Plate. Vol. I, Pl. I, p. 13.

Paris, Musée du Louvre.

XLVI. VIGÉE-LEBRUN, Elisabeth-Louise (1755–1842)

HEAD OF A YOUNG GIRL

Pastel and blue chalk

278 : 205

Exh: Paris: 'Exposition des Portraits des Femmes Peintres du XVIIIe Siècle' 1935 (8).

Paris, Musée du Louvre.

XLVII. BOCQUET, Pierre-Jean (1751–1817)

A COSTUME STUDY—A CHINAMAN DANCING

Watercolour

175 : 095

Paris, Bibliothèque de l'Opéra.

XLVIII. DAVID, Jacques-Louis

A STUDY FOR 'LE SACRE': NAPOLEON CROWNING HIMSELF

Black stone

292 : 252

Signed on the bottom: *L. David f.*

Coll: Millet; Cottenet (Sale, Paris 1917); Louvre, RF 4377.

Exh: Paris, Petit Palais: 'Gros, ses Amis, ses Elèves', 1936 (537); Zurich, Kunsthaus: 'Zeichnungen französischer Meister von David zu Millet', 1937 (64, Pl. I).

Lit: Jules David: *Le Peintre Louis David*, Paris 1880, p. 660; *L'Art Vivant*, 15.12.1925; L. Cantinelli: *Jacques-Louis David*, Paris-Bruxelles 1930, Pl. LXVI; M. Serullaz: *Quatorze Dessins de J. L. David* (Collection des reproductions de dessins publiés sous la direction de Gabriel Rouches, IX), Paris 1939, No. 5.

First sketch for the painting. There are differences between the drawing and painting. In this drawing, the Emperor crowns himself with his right hand and presses a sword to his breast with his left hand. In the picture, the Emperor holds the crown in both hands to place on the Empress's head and bless Pope Pius VII with a raised right hand. An old studio model served as the model for the Pope. A drawing for his picture of a nude man holding in his hands a globe surmounted by a cross, was in the Henri Rouart Sale, Paris 1912 (Vol. II, No. 67).

Paris, Musée du Louvre.

XLIX. CHARDIN, Jean-Baptiste Siméon (1699–1779)
LA VINAIGRETTE, LOUIS XV
Black chalk
284 : 405
Inscr. *Chardin*

Coll: Tessin. Bought by Tessin for one franc: see 'Note de Dessins à la Main, achetés à Paris, 1739, 1740, 1741' (Erik Muttmark's archives).
Exh: Stockholm, National Museum: 'Carl Gustaf Tessins Franska Handteckningar' (12); London, Burlington House, French Exhibition, 1932 (764 : 622 (Plate CLXXI); Paris, Galerie des Beaux-Arts 1935: 'Le Dessin français dans les Collections du XVIIIe Siècle' (56); Copenhagen: 'L'Art français au XVIIIe Siècle', 1935 (332); Paris, Palais National des Arts: 'Chefs d'Oeuvre de l'Art français' (520).
Lit: Schönbrunner—Meder, Vol. VIII, Pl. 914; Ernst Goldschmidt: *J. B. S. Chardin*, Stockholm 1945, Fig. XIII.
Presumably a preparatory sketch for Chardin's signboard of 'Un Chirurgien pansant dans sa Boutique un Homme blessé d'un Coup d'Epée', which was painted for one of Chardin's father's friends who was a surgeon. The original is lost: the preparatory sketch, after which Jules de Goncourt executed an etching, formerly hung in the Hotel de Ville, Paris, and was destroyed during the Commune in 1871. See Georges Wildenstein: *J. B. S. Chardin*, Paris 1933. No. 1226. Jules de Goncourt's etching is reproduced by Wildenstein, p. 153.
The drawing corresponds, with variants, to the print in reverse.
Stockholm, National Museum.

L. CHARDIN, Jean-Baptiste Siméon
SCENE AT AN INN
Red and black chalk heightened with white on grey-brown paper
280 : 370

Coll: Tessin (2962)
Exh: London, Burlington House: French Exhibition, 1932, (770 : 663).
Lit: Schönbrunner—Meder, Vol. VIII. Pl. 1008; Ernst Goldschmidt: *J. B. S. Chardin*. Stockholm 1945, Fig. XV.
This drawing may be compared with another sketch of a similar nature: 'L'Ecole', which was in the Michel-Lévy Sale, Paris 1919, p. 52, No. 71. (Plate).
Stockholm, National Museum.

LI. LANCRET, Nicolas (1690–1745)
STUDIES FOR 'LE DÉJEUNER AU JAMBON'
Red chalk
180 : 247

Coll: Anonymous Sale (London, Sotheby's, 22.3. 1923, 8).
Exh: Buffalo, Albright Art Gallery: 'Master Drawings', 1935 (62) Repr.
These are studies for Lancret's celebrated picture 'Le Déjeuner au Jambon', like its companion picture J. F. de Troys' 'Le Déjeuner d'Huîtres'. Both pictures are now in the Musée Condé, Chantilly.
A study of a valet opening a bottle, for the same picture, was in the collection of P. Defer. Dumesnil Sale, 1900 (168).
New York, Mrs I. C. Stralem.

LII. DURAMEAU, Louis Jacques (1733–1796)
THE CARD PARTY
Pencil on rose-coloured paper, washed with bistre and touched with white gouache
170 : 230
Signed: *Du Rameau*, 1767.

Coll: E. de Goncourt (Sale, Paris 1897, No. 70); Leon Michel-Lévy (1925, No. 49).
Exh: Paris: 'Exposition de petits Maîtres du XVIIIe Siècle', 1920 (268); Galerie des Beaux-Arts: 'Exposition E. et J. de Goncourt', 1933 (190); Paris, Palais National des Arts: 'Chefs d'Oeuvre de l'Art français', 1937 (530).
Lit: E. de Goncourt: *La Maison d'un Artiste*, 1881, Vol. I, pp. 72–73; *Les Maîtres du Dessin*, Vol. III, 1902, Pl. CXXII.

A drawing of the same subject (pen and chinese ink, 170 : 225) signed and dated 1777 was exhibited at the Musée Carnavalet: 'La Vie Parisienne au XVIIIe Siècle' 1928 (150), and was then in the collection of Mme de Ganay.

A slighter drawing in black pencil touched up with white chalk, resembling this composition, is also known. It was formerly in the Jules Masson Collection, and was exhibited in Paris: 'Petits Maîtres du XVIIIe Siècle' 1920 (271). It was later in the possession of Louis Godefroy, and was reproduced in his catalogue 'Estampes et Dessins', 1924 (198), Plate.

Paris, Musée du Louvre.

LIII. FRAGONARD, Jean Honoré
LE VERROU
Sepia with light touches of watercolour and bistre
240 : 350

Coll: Walferdin, 1880 (212): Josse; A. Beurdeley, 1905 (63); E. Kann (122); A. Meyer, 1935 (24); Meyer Sale, 1938 (8).
Exh: Paris, Jacques Seligmann, 1931: 'Dessins de Fragonard' (19).
Lit: Baron R. Portalis: *Honoré Fragonard*, Paris 1889, p. 314.
Engr. by Blott, 1784.

The same subject (240 : 270), from the collection Varanchan, 1777, was in the collection of Baron Edmond de Rothschild. Paintings of the same subject exist; one was in the Veri Sale 1785 (37).

Paris, private collection.

LIV. BAUDOUIN, Pierre-Antoine (1723–1769)
LE FRUIT DE L'AMOUR SECRET
Black chalk and stump with washes of indian ink
295 : 360

Coll: La Beraudière (Sale 1883, 3); Muhlbacher (Sale 1899, 68); Michel-Lévy (Sale 1920, 126); Albert Meyer (Cat. 1935, No. 1).
Exh: Paris, Musée Carnavalet: 'La Vie Parisienne au XVIIIe Siècle', 1928 (105); London, Burlington House: French Exhibition, 1932 (789 : 638).
Lit: G. Bourcaud: *Dessins, Gouaches, Estampes, Tableaux du XVIIIe Siècle*. Paris 1893, pp. 28–29.
First conception of the composition in gouache exhibited at the Salon 1767 and engraved in 1777 by Voyez Le Jeune (Bocher: *Les Gravures françaises au XVIIIe Siècle*. Paris 1875–1882, II, No. 23).

Another sketch of this subject is in the Louvre (23699). Another version was in 1931 in the K. E. Maison Gallery, Berlin.

Two fully worked-up gouaches were in the Collections of Baronne Edmond de Rothschild and M Arthur Veil-Picard.

Paris, private collection.

LV. PORTAIL, Jacques-André (1695–1759)
LE DUO
Pencil and red chalk
285 : 205

Exh: Paris, Musée de l'Orangerie: 'Les Chefs d'Oeuvre des Collections français retrouvés en Allemagne', 1946 (108).

Portail drawings of musicians are numerous. Another 'Duet' consisting of a 'cellist and a singer was in an Anonymous Sale (Paris, Hotel Drouot, 1899). In the eighteenth century, Portail's drawings were believed to be by Watteau. They reappeared under his own name in 1820, in the Silvestre Sale (69 drawings), then in that of his grandson in 1857.

Goncourt appreciated them but said they had not 'cette belle audace, même dans la maladresse, qu'ont parfois Pater et Lancret'.

Paris, private collection.

LVI. VINCENT, François-André (1746–1816)
THE PAINTER HALL AND HIS WIFE, NÉE GOBIN
Wash and bistre
375 : 325
Signed and dated: *Vincent*, 1771 or 1777

Exh: Paris, Musée Carnavalet: 'La Suède et Paris', 1947 (533).

The same portrait, painted in oil by Vincent with the possible collaboration of Fragonard, was exhibited in the 'Exposition Fragonard', Paris, 1921, as No. 49 'La Leçon de Dessin'. The picture was exhibited in the Salon of 1777 and was sketched by Gabriel de Saint-Aubin, in his *Catalogues de Ventes et Livrets du Salon*, ed. E. Dacier, Paris 1909, Vol. I, p. 53.

Paris, private collection.

LVII. DOYEN, Gabriel François (1726–1806)
A STUDY FOR 'LE MIRACLE DES ARDENTS OU SAINTE GENEVIÈVE DES ARDENTS'
Sepia
335 : 240

Inscr. on the mount: *Le Peste des Ardents, qui se manifeste à Paris l'an* 1100. *Première composition du tableau de Doyen que l'on voit à Paris dans l'Eglise à St Roch.*

A sketch for the painting in the Eglise Saint Roch in Paris, which was exhibited at the Musée Galliéra, 1946, 'Peinture méconnue des Eglises de Paris', No. 20, pp. 15–16. The painting was engraved by Normand. Another sketch is in the Louvre. (Guiffrey—Marcel, Vol. V, No. 260.) A sketch in grisaille, probably made for the engraving, is in the Musée Carnavalet and another in oil on paper is in the Louvre (Reiset, No. 713).

According to the catalogue of the exhibition at the Musée Galliéra, the painting was commissioned for the transept of the Eglise Saint Roch and exhibited in the Salon of 1767 (67).

The miracle occurred in the reign of Louis VI in 1129 when a pestilence which swept Paris was stopped owing to the intercession of Sainte Geneviève.

Drawings by this artist are exceedingly rare; see K. T. Parker: *Catalogue of the Drawings in the Ashmolean Museum, Oxford.* Oxford 1938, Vol. I, No. 487.

Bayonne, Musée Bonnat.

LVIII. NATOIRE, Charles-Joseph (1700–1777)
INTERIOR OF THE FRENCH ACADÉMIE IN ROME
520 : 330

Signed and dated: *C. Natoire 1745*

On the reverse is an inscription in Xavier Atger's hand: '*Intérieur de l'Ecole de l'Académie de Peinture à Rome*', *dessiné par Mr. Natoire, directeur des pensionnaires de France. Natoire est assis, et corrige les dessins de ses élèves. On voit sur les murs de l'intérieur* '*La famille de Darius aux pieds d'Alexandre*' *par Lebrun,* '*La maladie d'Alexandre*' *par Lesueur, et* '*La descente de Croix*' *par Jouvenet.*

Natoire, who had studied in Rome from 1723 to 1728, became Director of the French Académie at Rome in 1751. His administration was unsuccessful; he quarrelled with his students and resigned his position in 1774. He went to live in Castelgondolfo. A large collection of his landscape drawings is also in the Musée Atger at Montpellier.

Montpellier, Musée Atger.

LIX. DESPORTES, François (1661–1743)
A SELF-PORTRAIT
Red chalk
153 : 186

Lit: F. Reiset: No. 711; Guiffrey-Marcel, Vol. V, No. 3629.

First sketch for Desportes' painting in the Louvre: the right-hand side of the drawing (a dog and a horse) does not appear in the painting which has other variants.

Paris, Musée du Louvre.

LX. PRUD'HON, Pierre-Paul (1758–1823)
JOSEPHINE
Black stone heightened with white
The measurements of this drawing are not now available.

Exh: Rouen: 'Napoleon et son Temps' (112).

Another drawing of Josephine, on a bench at Malmaison, is in the Louvre (Don Camondo).

'Si Prud'hon ne fut pas le peintre official de la nouvelle Cour, il en fut au moins le peintre intime; il fut le portraitiste ordinaire et familier des femmes de la famille Impériale. A lui, revenait l'honneur de peindre l'Impératrice Josephine dans le frais décor de la Malmaison. On retrouve, dans les collections, des études, des esquisses, des ébauches à l'huile, toutes sortes de projets de portraits de la Reine Hortense, et des soeurs de l'Empereur.' E. J. de Goncourt.

Paris, private collection.

LXI. GILLOT, Claude (1673–1722)
LA MORT DE MAÎTRE ANDRÉ
Pen, red chalk and bistre wash
159 : 215

Inscr: 16 at the bottom.

Coll: Mariette.

Lit: Guiffrey—Marcel, Vol. VI, No. 4194; B. Populus: *Claude Gillot (1673–1722); Catalogue de l'Oeuvre gravé,* Paris 1930 (344); J. Poley: *Claude Gillot: Leben und Werk (1673–1722).* Würzburg 1938.

Engr: Huquier: *Livre de scènes comiques inventées par Gillot.*

The subject of this drawing is taken from Act II, Scene I of 'La Fausse Coquette', a comedy in three acts played by the Italian Comedians on December 18th, 1694. This play is attributed to Bruquéres de Barante and printed in the *Théâtre Italien* by Gherardi.

In all probability, Gillot executed his drawing after a later performance of this play by the Marionettes of the Théâtre de la Foire in about 1710–1715, while the Italian Comedians were exiled from Paris.

It should perhaps be stressed that the scene is not taken from the play of the same name, 'Le Tombeau de Maître André' after which Gillot also executed drawings, now in the Louvre.

Paris, Musée du Louvre.

LXII. SAINT-AUBIN, Gabriel Jacques de

RÉUNION SOUS LES ORANGERS
Black and white chalk on grey paper
256 : 316

Inscr. '*Palais du Régent, fête de Saint Louis*', 1754. *A porter à August . . . qu'il y mette la suitte* (?) . . . and some illegible words.

Coll: Hippolyte Destailleur (Paris, 27.4.1868, No. 205); Armand Valton.

Exh: Paris, Galerie Charpentier: 'Les Saint-Aubin', 1925 (25); London, Burlington House: French Exhibition, 1932 (800 : 748); Paris, Ecole des Beaux-Arts: 'Art français des XVIIe et XVIIIe Siècles', 1933 (150); Copenhagen: 'L'Art français du XVIIIe Siècle', 1935 (503); Paris: 'Chefs d'Oeuvre de l'Art français', 1937.

Lit: E. J. de Goncourt: *L'Art français du XVIIIe Siècle*, 1880, 438; P. Lavallée: 'La Collection de Dessins de l'Ecole des Beaux-Arts', *Gazette des Beaux-Arts*, 1917, p. 427 (Plate); P. Lavallée: *Dessins du XVIIIe Siècle à l'Ecole des Beaux-Arts*, 1928, p. 54, Pl. 27; E. Dacier: *Gabriel de Saint-Aubin*, Paris 1931, Vol. II, No. 662.

According to Pierre Lavallée, the inscriptions on the reverse are not in the artist's hand, and the identifications are of doubtful authenticity: even the date 1754 is questionable, and the costumes appear to be those of 1760–1765.

Paris, Ecole des Beaux-Arts.

LXIII. LAGRENÉE, Louis Jean François

(1725–1805)
THE PAINTER IN HIS STUDIO
Watercolour
250 : 335

Exh: Paris, Musée Carnavalet: 'La Vie Parisienne au XVIIIe Siècle', 1928 (181).

This is a self-portrait of the artist in his studio. While few self-portraits of artists exist in the sixteenth century and even in the seventeenth century, many artists of the eighteenth century, Chardin, Jeaurat, Lepicié, portrayed not only the *rapin* (the small draughtsman at work) but also the painter in his studio, which was to become a frequent theme in nineteenth-century painting.

Paris, private collection.